Given by

Tri-County Arts and Crafts Guild

October 2002

THE ART OF THROWING

The Art of Throwing

Alex McErlain

The Crowood Press

First published in 2002 by
The Crowood Press Ltd
Ramsbury, Marlborough
Wiltshire SN8 2HR

British Library Cataloguing-in-Publication Data
A catalogue record for this book is available from the British Library.

ISBN 1 86126 484 4

Photographs by Stephen Yates except where otherwise stated.
Line artwork by Keith Field.

Photograph previous page: Saltglazed pitcher by Alex McErlain.
Height 25cm (9.8in). Stoneware 2001.

Designed and typeset by Annette Findlay

Printed and bound in Singapore by Craft Print International Ltd.

Contents

Acknowledgements

I wish to acknowledge all those who have helped and encouraged me in the preparation of this book. Most importantly I must thank my wife and family for their patience and understanding throughout the period of writing. Stephen Yates, who took most of the photographs, worked with diligence and sensitivity to produce visual material that is clear and communicative. My tutors, Derek Emms and Ray Finch, left me a legacy of knowledge that underpins the entire volume.

My colleagues at Manchester Metropolitan University have played a central role in supporting me throughout the task. I have probably learnt as much from my students during twenty-five years of teaching as they have learnt from me: it's a two-way process. The historical examples illustrated belong to the decorative arts collection of MMU, as do some of the contemporary works.

I must thank all the potters who over the years have willingly shared their knowledge and experience, enabling me to deepen my understanding. Thank you to those who gave permission for their work to be used in illustration. Rosemary Cochrane helped to initiate the book; Will Levi Marshall and Kate Bartle must be thanked for their co-operation in demonstrating composite pots. A particular mention must go to Jim Malone, whose friendship has given me much support; and to the late Patrick Sargent, who had a profound effect on my understanding of the art of throwing.

This book is dedicated to all those unknown potters from throughout history, whose work continues to enrich the lives of so many.

Introduction

'To speak a foreign language
in your own tongue.

No, not just one
but a number of languages.

Korean. Old English.
Mineral. Manual.

The different and difficult
dialects of fire.'

From *Hidden Syntax* by Christopher Reid.

The complexities of the art of throwing are masked by the simple communicative nature of pots. Throwing is an art, an expressive art; moreover it is the primary means of visual communication of some people. Like other artists, potters must become immersed in their art to achieve the highest levels of communication; but unlike some other arts, pottery is not transient, but permanent – and with this permanency comes a formidable responsibility.

This book has grown from my passion for thrown pots, for buying them, using them, discussing them, and most of all for making them. The chapters on how to make pots have been developed from many years spent teaching students how to begin, progressively challenging them with greater complexities of design and skill acquisition until they have the confidence to continue the learning process unaided.

Other chapters reflect the nature of my discussions with those who share my passion for communicating about pots, because it is this that makes an exhibition opening so lively; and when a pot is purchased and taken home to be used, inevitably that communication continues, albeit silently.

Recently I was waiting with Takeshi Yasuda who was about to address a conference: when asked by a delegate if he were nervous, Takeshi assured us that he was not: 'It's only words, after all, and they disappear into the air; it is when I sit at the wheel to throw, then I am nervous!' he said.

There are pots illustrated in this book that were made over two thousand years ago, and we are still examining and learning from the language of expression used by those very same potters.

1 The Inspirational Past

Pottery-making flourished for many centuries before the first wheel-thrown pots appeared. The region known as 'Mesopotamia' in the Middle East produced some of the first thrown pots from around 3000BC. Mesopotamia lies between two rivers, the Tigris and the Euphrates, and these regularly flood the surrounding lands, depositing layers of a rich plastic clay suitable for throwing. Early thrown pots would have been made on a slow-turning wheel, probably made of stone, until the technology was refined and fast wheels became the norm. In the five thousand years that have passed since the first thrown pots were made, many civilizations have developed thrown ware, providing us with an enormous inspirational resource from which to study and learn.

With so much thrown pottery available, it is an impossible task to make a comprehensive analysis within the scope of this chapter; nevertheless, there are certain classic periods and civilizations that it is important to study in order to make a start at what will inevitably become a lifetime's work delving into the publications and collections that document the history of throwing.

Early Thrown Pottery

In 1937 archeologists discovered the remains of a potter's workshop in Palestine that contained pots, together with some tools and materials showing evidence of throwing. The remains were dated to 1200BC, and provided clear evidence of the mode of manufacture, borne out by examining the pots themselves. The tools included shaped pottery ribs, exactly like the ribs used today, and there were also polishing stones and shells, together with a bone probably used as an incising or cutting tool. The component parts of a wheel-bearing made from basalt provided evidence of the sophisticated level of equipment used by these potters.

A good account of the excavation and the discoveries made appears in *Pottery in the Making* by Freestone & Gaimster. The pots that were discovered show the way in which a range of forms was explored, including a composite flask decorated with concentric circles painted whilst the vessel was supported on a revolving wheel. Similar characteristics may be seen in the pot with banded decoration from Cyprus (*see* illustration below).

The plethora of finely thrown pottery produced in Cyprus around 1300BC was made from buff-coloured clay with slip decoration painted in red and black. Banding was a favoured decorative technique, indicating the

OPPOSITE:

Jordanian flasks. Height 26cm (10in). Earthenware; unglazed. 300BC. These sensitively thrown flasks demonstrate the sophisticated skills that were possible with early wheel technology.

Ewer made in Cyprus. Height 19cm (7.5in). Fine buff clay painted with iron. Turned foot-ring, 600–400BC.

ease with which wheels could be controlled: the wheel makes fine banding possible, and many early thrown pots developed decoration using this technique. The absence of glaze for early pottery led potters to develop a palette of colours and textures that exploited the available clays and minerals. Most clays are brown or buff in colour, and by mixing differing clays and adding iron, the most commonly available metal oxide, potters produced a range of ware that was stylistically distinctive.

Mesopotamia

The wide range of pottery made in Mesopotamia included some particularly fine wares known as eggshell-ware bowls, from Ur in the south. These bowls were made during the fifth to the fourth centuries BC and are very finely thrown, their typical characteristics – that have led to them being called 'eggshell wares' – showing a concern for precision and tautness of form. The curvature of a typical bowl clearly describes an uninterrupted linear movement, completed by a thinned rim that reinforces the feeling of strength with delicacy, such as is associated with eggshells. Similar concerns have also been pursued by many twentieth-century potters who have associated their work with the modernist movement.

There is still much to be learnt from those early potters from Mesopotamia and their products, these all developed with a limited range of materials and equipment.

Ancient Greece

The wheel was first used in Greece during 2000BC. In the sixth century, Athens was the centre of production for the finest black figure-painted vases ever made. The clay for making the pots was of a red earthenware type, fine grained and dense when fired, and a type of slip called *terra sigillata* was used to decorate them. This slip is made up of particles of the finest size, arrived at through a process known as levigation: in this process a container is filled with slip that is then allowed to settle; the heaviest particles will settle at the bottom, and the upper layer, where the finest particles remain, is removed; the fine slip is then subjected to further levigation, until a small quantity of extremely fine-particled slip remains. This slip, when applied and burnished, produces a layer on the surface of the pot that shines like glaze when fired.

Fine slip allowed potters to make very delicate and intricate decoration, and the vessels produced to carry such decoration had characteristics that could best exploit this potential: curved, open bowl forms of uninterrupted line, large amphorae with thrown feet, and straight-walled vases.

Signatures appeared on pots from 700BC; for instance 'Sophilos' and 'Exekias' both signed their wares. Some pots had drawings of their method of manufacture on them, so we have evidence of the type of wheel used. Also the colour range of black and red made the ware particularly distinctive. Greek pots were heavily and precisely worked in order to provide the most suitable vehicle for decoration; but because of this their form is sometimes considered stilted, mannered and lifeless.

The pots are particularly worth studying if you wish to learn about proportional relationships and the infinite range of possibilities for subdividing form with decoration. Mathematical proportional division is incorporated in many amphorae, the decorative linear subdivisions unifying the proportions of the component parts of the form.

Crete

The island of Crete was a production centre for fine thrown wares in a wide range of bold forms. Enormous storage jars made in Knossos date back as far as 1400BC; their form and scale are imposing, the decorative applied bands of clay dominate, and the methods of construction through coil and throw have been inspirational to many studio potters.

With large-scale pots, the rhythmic movements of the form must be developed with certainty; but controlling these larger pots on the wheel demands decisiveness if the potter is to remain in control of the spinning wet clay. The process of building up the pot in stages is relatively slow, therefore changes are not easily incorporated, and a good vision of the completed form is necessary throughout construction. Studying the many ways in which Cretan potters enliven a large expanse of form without making it look fiddly teaches us a great deal about the conception and development of an idea.

The Roman Empire

The Romans learned how to throw pots in a very smooth clay body that they then covered in a fine slip. This type of pottery was known as Samian ware: it was oxidized-fired, a process that produced a distinctive red colour, and it dominated all Roman pottery production. Samian ware may be described as Roman tableware made in very fine red earthenware clay, coated with a layer of *terra sigillata* slip that fires to a glossy surface. Samian ware was used throughout the Roman Empire from the late first century BC to the early fourth century AD.

One method of making Samian ware is by throwing clay into a mould that has been fixed to the potter's wheel; the inside of the mould was often carved with a decoration that picked up on the outside of the bowl, enabling the mass production of a decorative pot. Indeed, the production of Roman pottery was undertaken on such a scale, and shards have been excavated that record manufacturing quantities in excess of 25,000 vessels. The ware was frequently decorated by using stamps and rollers, which brought uniformity with speed.

The methodologies of the ancient Romans have certainly influenced contemporary industrial manufacture, that today uses machinery to make pots on a mould fixed to a revolving wheel. Some studio potters have found inspiration from the Roman methods of production, that allow an individual to manufacture work on a significant scale whilst retaining an element of individual creative input. For instance, the feet on Samian-ware pots are particularly interesting to examine, the form bold, and cut with precision to a scale that is large in relation to the overall proportion of the object.

Finally, the Roman potters appreciated the characteristics that throwing produced, and whilst not emphasizing throwing lines, they did not seek to eliminate them completely, rather working the surface finely, to complement the cut and the moulded treatment.

The Islamic World

The extensive pottery production of Islam, a world that stretched from the borders of India in the east to North Africa and Spain in the west, is characterized by the use of glaze and colour. Influences from China – the consequence of trading – inspired Islamic potters to develop glazed wares. Particularly notable are lustre-painted pots: this was a technique developed for glassware, but when used with pottery,

*R*oman Samian ware.

Flask made in Alexandria. Height 22cm (8.6in). Earthenware, red clay with white slip and a clear glaze.

meant that it could be made in imitation of more expensive metal wares. Islamic pottery is made of low-fired earthenware that enables a bright colour response from the metal oxides. The pottery was highly valued; characteristic forms include water flasks, spouted jugs and elaborately decorated bowls.

The development of decoration on a circular bowl form is much studied and prized today; the range of patterns produced is extensive, and the spirit with which the decoration is painted varies from the free and casual to the precise and careful. Lustre-painted bowls from ninth-century Iraq contain intense and spirited painted decoration that some studio potters have found particularly inspirational. Especially worthy of study are the many ways in which the rims of bowls and plate forms are treated. Because the rim frames a circular form, it needs careful consideration when painted decoration is the intention, and Islamic potters approached this problem in many creative ways. Thus sometimes the form of the rim was used to establish a border, and at other times it contributed to the development of designs that moved from the centre of the plate outwards, across the rim itself.

The Far East

China

China has produced some of the world's finest pottery, and advances in ceramic technology in China mostly pre-date other civilizations; therefore we see the Chinese producing the first high-fired, glazed stoneware and porcelain that other countries strove to emulate. The first wheel-made pottery was unglazed, thin-walled, and often developed in imitation of the characteristics of bronze vessels. By the time of the Han dynasty (221BC–AD220) glazed ware was in regular production, both earthenware with lead glaze and stoneware using ash glaze being made. It is the early ash-glazed stonewares that have had a profound influence on contemporary Western potters, the most notable forms being jars and tall-necked bottles usually featuring a layer of ash glaze that was visually and sometimes physically contained within raised bands of clay. The glaze was composed principally of ash from the kiln together with clay,

and was green in colour; and when reduced fired, it contrasted well with the warm colours of the clay body.

The visual image is of boldness and strength, the relationship of form to glaze intimate. The potters frequently made wares that were deceptively uncontrolled; for instance, jars with raised bands had notches cut in them to allow molten glaze to escape and run down the form in an apparently uncontrolled fashion – although the Chinese potters appreciated the contribution that the kiln made to the overall design of the pot. It is this early respect for the 'casual' appearance that has attracted modern potters, who have sought to emulate those characteristics within their own wares.

THE TANG DYNASTY, 618–906

Pottery production in the Tang dynasty was dominated by glazed earthenware in three colours: this was known as sancei ware. During this period, the lead frit from which glazes are made began to be imported from the West, and potters learned to use to their advantage the brilliance that lead brings to coloured glaze: green, brown and clear glazes were intermixed on finely thrown forms. Tang pots are characterized by their bulbous shape, their curves suggestive of natural form, with slender neck and finely detailed rim, and their form has been of notable influence – furthermore, the translucent nature of lead glaze highlights the nuances of pottery form. The particularly refined and delicate characteristics of these pots demand precision in the manner in which the clay is handled on the wheel.

Contemporary potters have studied these pots, and have explored the language of throwing with intense concentration to try and capture some of the precision inherent within Tang dynasty pots.

THE SONG DYNASTY, 960–1279

The twentieth-century artist potter Bernard Leach regarded Song dynasty pottery as being of such high quality that it might usefully be employed as a standard by which other pottery could be measured or compared. Leach pointed out the 'use of natural colours and textures in clays, the quality of their glazes, the beauty and vitality of their well balanced and proportioned forms' as a source of inspiration. Song pots are characterized by their primary concern with form, although many were also extensively decorated. The pots are generally curvaceous, with one movement flowing into another, and their glaze was developed to highlight the strengths of the form.

Celadon wares were glazed with pale green and blue-green coloured glazes, and are particularly notable. The characteristics of celadon glaze may be observed in carved or fluted bowls, where the raised surface is exploited to thin the glaze, and the deep recessed areas to develop darker colour. Celadon glaze is translucent, therefore the colour and surface of the pot may be seen through the glaze.

In contrast to celadon wares that were often quite thickly potted, the ding wares of the twelfth century are made in ivory-white porcelain, extremely thinly potted and sometimes finely carved. Ding ware has a kind of skeletal form, thus shortcomings cannot be concealed, so the potting must be assured if it is not to

appear contrived. The foot-rings on ding wares have been studied for their fine, sensitive turning and the elegance they contribute to the form. Some ding-ware bowls were fired upside down, the foot glazed all over, and the rim left unglazed, perhaps to be mounted with a fine metal band.

Small bowls were made in south China for domestic use, and these came to be admired by the Japanese tea masters who imported them for the tea ceremony. The black glaze known as 'temmoku' was applied thickly to a substantial form. The glaze is characterized by its dense and sometimes pitted surface that contrasts with a rich brown colour developed in areas where the glaze is thin – for example, on the rim or a sharp edge. Temmoku bottles appear stark and austere in comparison to celadon wares; they have a pronounced emphasis on form, and have been of enormous influence to the studio pottery movement.

Tea bowl, Chinese Sung dynasty. Width 11cm (4in). Stoneware with black temmoku glaze; twelfth century.

Cizhou wares are characterized by decoration – either brushwork or sgraffito through black glaze. The stoneware jars produced during the twelfth to the thirteenth centuries carry elaborate and freely drawn decorative motifs, much admired for the bold manner in which they were executed. Cizhou pots were made for everyday use rather than specifically for the court, and it is the bold and seemingly carefree manner in which the pots were thrown, placing emphasis on the inherent qualities of the making process, that was to have a profound influence on studio potters.

THE MING DYNASTY, 1368–1644

Ming dynasty pottery is principally known for the predominance of blue cobalt brush decoration. Imported cobalt from the Middle East was very pure in contrast to Chinese cobalt that produced softer hues. Cobalt is the strongest of the colouring oxides, and lends itself to the development of fine, linear decoration. In the twentieth century it was the pottery painted with impure cobalt, often applied to everyday wares, that inspired studio potters.

THE QUING DYNASTY, 1644–1911

Pottery from the Quing dynasty is characterized by elaborate surface decoration, largely regarded as deeply unfashionable by studio potters. Enamel painting is undertaken with a coloured, low temperature glaze, applied to the surface of a glazed and fired pot. The low firing temperature allows the development of bright, intense colours, and the fired glaze surface provides a ground that can be worked with confidence. One studio potter who used enamel painting frequently was Shoji Hamada, who sought to combine the glaze values of earlier periods with bright, overglaze enamels.

Plate, Chinese Ming dynasty. Width 26cm (10in). Stoneware made from a fine buff clay and decorated with impure cobalt, the brushwork describing baskets of foliage. The centre of the dish has an unglazed ring so that another dish can be fired whilst standing inside. Fifteenth century.

Korea

Pottery from Korea and other countries in south-east Asia, such as Thailand, has been particularly influential in the West. Some of the earliest thrown pottery appeared in the Silla period, 50BC–AD935, when the potter's wheel was introduced from China. It was during the Koryo dynasty, 935–1392, that inlaid celadon wares became popular, their soft, contoured forms complemented by greyish-green glaze exposing crisp patterns in black and white inlay. During the Yi dynasty (1392–1910), two types of ware predominated: the Punchong, literally 'powder green' or greyish-green, slip-decorated stonewares made until the late sixteenth century; and plain white porcelain that satisfied the rather more austere taste of the Korean.

This porcelain was of such high quality that Chinese envoys would take it for presentation to the emperor. Bernard Leach purchased a white porcelain full moon jar of the Choson dynasty (seventeenth to eighteenth century), now in the British museum; he regarded it as an outstanding example of austere, asymmetric form, and he spent a lot of time promoting the validity of this conviction to others. Japanese tea masters collected simple Korean bowls for use in the tea ceremony, valuing their unsophisticated characteristics and expressive form.

Japan

The potter's wheel was introduced into Japan from Korea during the fifth century. Japanese ceramics were notably influential in the twentieth century, principally because of the promotion of Eastern pottery by Bernard Leach. The values that the Japanese like to see in pottery place emphasis on asymmetric form and natural glaze firing; for example, the rough qualities of Shigaraki ware – that have been much admired – came about as a result of an extended firing in an anagama kiln.

In this process, the ash from the burning fuel is deposited on unprotected wares and forms a natural glaze, the thickness of which depends on how the flames pass through the chamber. Tamba ware has also had considerable influence, inspiring publications that focus not just on the pottery itself, but on the spirit of its production.

Perhaps the most influential of all Japanese ceramic wares is raku, a type of low temperature pottery principally associated with the tea ceremony. In *A Potter's Book*, Bernard Leach describes how his interest in pottery was awakened by a raku firing, and this effectively gave worldwide promotion to the technique.

Also noteworthy is the role of the Mingei movement in promoting values that are integral to everyday objects; this in turn led to the recognition of a wide range of wares made throughout the world in rural communities.

Particularly influential has been the recognition of the values inherent within the products of a society whose concerns are for the appropriateness of materials and purpose; Soyetsu Yanagi and Shoji Hamada played an important part in the promotion of this philosophy.

India

India is home to a million potters and has a long tradition of throwing; indeed, many pots are still thrown on a variety of momentum wheels today – cartwheels, for example, are commonly adapted for throwing, the weight distribution making them act as a fly-ring. The potters squat alongside the wheel to throw, though they may stand up to set it in motion,

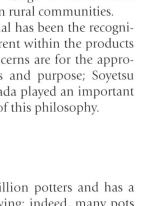

OPPOSITE:

Lidded jar, Chinese Quing dynasty. Height 38cm (15in). White stoneware, decorated with enamels. Eighteenth century.

Jar made in Shigaraki, Japan. Height 30cm (12in). Mizugame heian-style, wood-fired. Twentieth century.

using a long stick that they insert into the rim. In the last few years there has been a growth in publications about Indian pottery, until recently a severely neglected area. The study of wheel technology will reveal much about the techniques possible, starting from very simple stone wheels whose forebears may be traced right back to earliest times.

The predominant ceramic tradition throughout India is low-fired, unglazed terracotta. The pots are frequently decorated with linear patterns drawn in slip.

The wheel is used to make not only an extensive range of practical items such water-carrying pots, grain holders and roof tiles, but also sculptures and figurines. For example, a model horse is thrown with a bottle-shaped pot to form its middle, with thrown legs attached; such horses are used for ceremonial purposes, and are produced in quantity. The skill with which Indian potters adapt composite thrown forms to develop fluent and lively animal shapes has had a big influence on Western potters.

North America

By 1600, Devonshire pots were being exported to the United States of America. Glazes and the potter's wheel were never invented in pre-Colombian America, so the introduction of wheel-making came via the immigrants from Europe who settled on the east coast. The products of these immigrant potters developed stylistically along the lines they had brought from their home country. But with the rapid expansion of the market for pottery came the development of new styles and a distinctive new language of expression. Earthenware was widely produced, and stoneware was in production from 1700.

The robust products of workshops from Pennsylvania and North Carolina have had a major influence on twentieth-century potters. Large storage jars were made in quantity and are particularly expressive in character. The scale of the pot often demanded the use of a throwing rib, a method that imparts a dense surface to a strong curvilinear form. Jars typically would have two handles and be decorated with splashes of glaze forming glassy drips running down the form.

But alongside the development of small-scale workshops ran factory production on an industrial scale, and this mirrored the new manufacturing technologies being developed in Europe. American pottery also developed a strand of art wares that centred on individual artists, such as George Ohr, together with groups of people whose concerns were primarily for decoration.

In the twentieth century America has produced a wealth of wheel-made pottery: this is largely due to the fact that it has a strong studio pottery movement with a particularly experimental emphasis, a pioneering educational system, and an unparalleled role in the promotion of throwing as a means of individual expression.

Europe

Spain

The wheel was established in Spain by 500BC. Centuries of production have established a characteristic Spanish style in which tin-glazed pottery predominates. Tin-glaze decoration was brought to Spain by medieval Islamic potters, and eventually spread via trade routes into Europe.

The most influential Spanish pottery has undoubtedly been decorated lustre ware: the pots are painted with a thin layer of metallic oxide, and fired in a reducing atmosphere to produce a metallic sheen. Lustre-ware production flourished during the fifteenth and sixteenth centuries. Large, wheel-formed vessels that can carry the intended decoration often feature thrown feet to create a pedestal effect. Handles are also a distinctive feature of large jars, and sometimes these are developed to such a scale that they dominate the form.

Italy

Tin-glazed earthenware became a popular medium for figurative painting in Renaissance Italy. Idealized heads that conformed to notions of beauty from that period were painted on plates. Tin glaze, or *majolica*, involves painting with oxides onto the unfired powdery glaze surface: this requires the potter to use bold brushstrokes that will still be visible when the pot is fired. The relationship of form to decoration was extensively explored by

OPPOSITE:

*J*ar by Cantigalli. *Height 37cm (14.5in). Red clay with white tin glaze and copper lustre; the tall foot-ring was thrown on. A copy of a sixteenth-century Hispano Moresque jar. Nineteenth century.*

Italian potters, and is particularly worth studying if you are planning to make painted wares.

Pottery form that is appropriate for tin-glaze painting would have broad, uninterrupted surfaces onto which brushwork may be applied.

The jar illustrated opposite has been painted with copper, cobalt and manganese oxides. Drug jars are shaped so they can be grasped when a row of them are placed together on a shelf. The fat rim may have been used to tie a cover on the jar.

When studying Italian pottery it is worthwhile reading an account of pottery-making published in 1557 and called *The Three Books of the Potter's Art*, by Cipriano Piccolpasso. The publication is extensively illustrated and documents all aspects of production.

Germany

The salt-glaze stoneware pottery produced in Germany from the sixteenth century has inspired many studio potters. Salt glazing is carried out by introducing common salt to the kiln when stoneware temperatures have been reached. Salt volatilizes at high temperature, the vapours travelling through the kiln and glazing the pots in the process. Salt glaze produces quite a thin layer of glaze, but it will enhance surface detail; consequently much of the ware relies on simple form decorated with bands, sgraffito lines and moulded sprigs.

The improvements to the production of ale in the sixteenth century led to increased consumption, and thence a demand for vessels to store and serve the drink: this was met by salt-glaze German pottery.

Narrow-necked, bulbous jars are the most common form; they sometimes carried the sprig-moulded head of a bearded man on the neck. These pots are known as *Bartmaske* bottles, though in Britain they were given the name Bellarmine, which is the one now commonly used. Salt-glaze pottery was sometimes used as ballast in ships trading from Holland to England.

Great Britain

The potter's wheel was used in Britain during the Roman occupation, however, its use eventually declined until the ninth century, when it was reintroduced by immigrant potters from Europe. The most influential group of historical wares from Britain are pots made in medieval times, and in particular jugs, with their strong visual language; these have had a profound effect on studio potters. The finest medieval pottery was made during the thirteenth and fourteenth centuries: tall, elegant forms were decorated by applying strips and pellets of clay, stamping, sgraffito and slip painting; they were then glazed with lead glazes, a process that produced a muted range of colours from yellow to green. Some jugs carried modelled animals and figures attached to the neck, a clear indication that the pots were intended to be visually entertaining and not just utilitarian. Bernard Leach was a passionate advocate of the qualities to be found in medieval pottery; his writings led to worldwide interest in, and appreciation of the genre.

OPPOSITE:

Italian tin-glazed drug jar. Height 26cm (10in).

Bellarmine made in Germany. Height 34cm (13.4in). Salt-glaze stoneware with brown slip; sprigs form the face and shield. Seventeenth century.

Cistercian wares were made in the north of England from the late fifteenth century: they included very finely potted drinking cups, made from red clay and glazed with a shiny dark brown glaze stained with manganese. Cistercian wares are notable for their fine pulled handles – sometimes there would be several handles on one vessel. The throwing is very precise, and contrasts starkly with the coarser nature of medieval forms.

English slipware made in the seventeenth and eighteenth centuries is characterized by its freedom of throwing and by the variety of decorative treatment in slip. Pots primarily served a domestic market and featured items for drinking, cooking and storage, together with some commemorative wares. During this period some notable potters signed their wares, for example Thomas Toft, whose large thrown chargers have become renowned. The chargers were usually fired standing upright on their edge, probably to prevent the dish from cracking, though possibly also for reasons of economy when setting the kiln. Whatever the reason, the firing process influenced the design of the form just as much as the decoration did.

The Wheel in Industry

The wheel played a significant role in the rise of pottery manufacture on an industrial scale: in Britain this industry developed in Staffordshire from the eighteenth century onwards. Factory wares eventually came to be dominated by mould-made wares, but many pots were thrown right through the nineteenth century. Industrial-thrown pottery is frequently characterized by its lathe-turned appearance. This is because pots were thrown slightly thicker than required to allow a lathe turner to shave the surface with precision in order to maintain uniformity. The individual character imparted by different throwers could in this way be eliminated, and another aesthetic emerged: lathe turning offers the possibility of making very fine linear bands in combination with a polished or burnished surface. The wheel was seen as a vehicle for speedy production, the only real disadvantage being that a skilled thrower was required.

The products of the pottery industry are largely mass-produced tablewares, but during the nineteenth century some manufacturers set up studios for the production of 'one-off' or limited edition art wares. Doulton & Company, a large manufacturer of utilitarian salt-glaze ware, set up an art studio in 1866 largely concerned with decorating the factory wares. Other manufacturers followed suit, and the products of these factory-based art studios in Britain and America became popular, thereby encouraging the industry to involve artists and designers to develop their ideas. Wheel-made vases, which were very popular, were thrown by one of the skilled factory workers to a design prepared by the artist. But this division of labour and creativity led to works that tended not to reflect the making process, and as a consequence, many studio potters regard them as lifeless.

Country Pottery

Whilst the mass production of pottery throughout Europe and America shifted towards industry and eventually away from throwing, there ran alongside it a strand of production that continued to be wheel-made right through until the twentieth century. This type of pottery was normally based in a rural environment and served the needs of a specialized community

where agriculture dominated. The products of country pottery are economic in design and manufacture, with little extraneous decoration. Plant pots often form the basis of the production, together with household items for storage and cooking.

The potteries developed products that used locally available materials – in fact, potteries were often established close to a clay and fuel source. Rural potteries frequently operated on a scale of production to keep twenty people employed, and had their own training methods to teach new employees how to throw. The apprentice system taught people about all aspects of manufacture, from digging clay to firing the kiln; throwers were expected to be fast and skilful, and the products reflected some of these requirements.

Thus the design of country ware reflects the way that forms evolve in response to the demands of use and the implications of the throwing process. Wheel design developed extensively during this period, which saw mechanization being harnessed to developing systems for powering the wheel.

Studio Pottery

During the twentieth century the number of individual artists who found expression through making pots grew to such an extent that they came to be identified as a movement known as 'studio pottery'. Indeed it continues to flourish, and many significant individuals have emerged from within its bounds and shaped its course.

It is not within the scope of this publication to try and define the extraordinary range of strands and developments that has shaped the studio pottery movement; however, it may be helpful to mention the work of a few practitioners who in their own way represent some points of significance.

Bernard Leach, 1887–1979

Bernard Leach had a profound influence on the development of the studio pottery movement through his work, his writing and his lecture

*R*hubarb forcing pot: *Greet potteries, Gloucestershire. 51cmw × 51cmh (20 × 20in). Earthenware. Late nineteenth century.*

tours. He initially learnt about pottery in Japan before settling in St Ives, England; here in 1920, he established the Leach Pottery, an enterprise that came to be known worldwide.

Leach made his own individual pots all through his life, but he also established the idea of a small group of potters working collectively to produce a range of tableware to a set design. The Leach Pottery took on students who stayed for a year or two before leaving to establish their own workshops; in this way therefore, its influence spread very quickly.

Leach's pots, taking their inspiration from both the East and West, were widely exhibited, and spawned many imitations, though these were usually of a poorer quality. However, it was the publication of *A Potter's Book* that did most to spread Leach's ideas about pots and pottery making. The book has never been out of print, and is considered a classic of its kind.

Michael Cardew, 1901–83

Cardew was Leach's pupil, and he proved to be an extraordinary figure in the development of the studio pottery movement. His passion was for English slipware, and he eventually established a centre and workshop for himself at Winchcombe in Gloucestershire, England, in what was originally a country pottery. The skill and passion with which he made pots inspired many followers. He published a book called *Pioneer Pottery*, after a time working in Africa where he founded a number of workshops; these were unique in that they relied entirely on

Pilgrim plate by Bernard Leach. Width 32cm (12.6in). Reduced stoneware. c. 1968.

Winchcombe pottery slipware; lidded jar and planter by Ray Finch; cereal bowl and small flagon by Michael Cardew; mustard pot by Charles Tustin. c. 1936.

his ability to identify, mine and process all the materials necessary to make pots.

Cardew's work is imbued with characteristics that derive from the making process. The pots take full advantage of the nature and behaviour of the materials used, and make no attempt to dissimulate the way they have evolved. It was this directness that was to have the most influence: it has been described as 'truth to materials', and many potters who were inspired by this attitude are still working today.

Cardew's pottery in Winchcombe was taken over by his most creative pupil, Ray Finch, and the pottery has been in continuous production ever since, playing an influential role of its own through its products, its philosophy, and its potential as a training ground for others.

Shoji Hamada, 1892–1978

Hamada began his career as a potter helping Bernard Leach to establish the pottery in St Ives. On his return to Japan he worked for the rest of his life in Mashiko, producing a range of new and visually exciting forms that feature a limited range of glazes.

Hamada was a central figure in the development of the Mingei movement that promoted the values of traditional folkcraft. He was one of the world's most notable artist potters, influencing people by way of his approach to throwing and by his lifestyle, as well as with the spirited work he produced. Typical Hamada pots celebrate the values of traditional ware in a thoroughly contemporary manner: thus a large,

shallow bowl with a sensitively detailed rim may have a layer of decorative glaze rapidly poured across the interior in a gestural movement, the lines and dribbles created forming shapes that complement the curves of the design.

Hamada was probably inadvertently responsible for the proliferation of tea bowls made by Western potters who had no direct association with the tea ceremony. It was in the tea bowls made by Hamada that Western potters saw most clearly the freedom with which he worked clay: his tea bowls are almost like drawings, boldly executed through a confident series of movements, and Western potters found that by emulating the spirit of their production they had a means by which to practise their creative skill. Thus it is not uncommon to hear potters saying that they begin a throwing cycle by making tea bowls as a means of loosening up, rather like a musician playing scales.

Hamada's tea bowls deserve extensive study as a way of learning how a simple form may be interpreted in many ways, without ever running out of ideas.

Hans Coper, 1920–81

Coper was a refugee from Germany who spent his potting life working in England. He was first introduced to potting by Lucie Rie, and their work is often stylistically linked. Coper's concerns were for the sculptural qualities inherent in wheel-thrown form, and he produced a limited range of shapes that were developed in series, usually finished in black or white, and with a finely textured surface.

Many of Coper's pots were composite forms, assembled from thrown parts in unusual configuration. The aesthetic character of his work was entirely modernist, betraying only a superficial influence from ancient sculpture. Coper taught many students at the Royal College of Art in London. Although it is unusual to see any directly influential reference in the work of others, his attitude to analytical thinking has left a profound legacy.

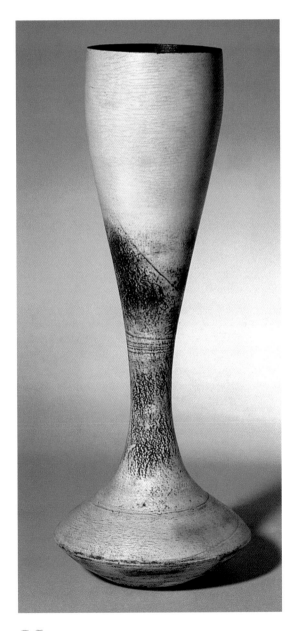

*H*our-glass vase by Hans Coper. Height 47cm (18.5in). Oxidized stoneware. 1967.

Peter Voulkos, b.1924

The most influential American potter of the late twentieth century is Peter Voulkos. His gestural wheel-made work was as much influenced by ideas from abstract expressionist painters as by the spirit inherent in the process of manipulating large-scale form. Coming from a background in painting, Voulkos explored the ways in which pots could be taken to extremes by stretching and manipulating whilst still retaining the characteristics associated with wheel movement. He inaugurated new ideas about how a vessel may be seen, especially in the context of historical precedent. His work may make reference to bottle, jar or plate, but the spirited rendition of the language of those forms takes on a whole new meaning.

Voulkos' work as a teacher at the Otis Art Institute and the University of California played a seminal role in the development of the studio pottery movement in America. He encouraged students to become totally involved in the making process and to use clay in an ambitious and spirited manner. The ideas he first explored had a great influence on the development of European ceramics, which up to that point had largely been concerned with more formal aspects of making. This cross-continental influence has been a predominant feature of late twentieth-century pottery.

A New Generation

The history of pottery is a continuing one: whilst some individuals shaped the initial studio pottery movement, it is the involvement of new generations that will shape the future. The movement is now firmly established worldwide, and practitioners move from country to country, culture to culture, shaping ideas that will influence and inspire future generations. There are many good potters whose work is influential; here, just a small selection of representatives has been chosen to show the range of ideas and interests currently being explored.

Walter Keeler, b.1942

Keeler epitomizes the potter whose fascination with history is manifested in expressly new work that references previous styles and interests.

Teapot by Walter Keeler. Height 21cm (8in). Salt-glaze stoneware. 1984.

He is just as likely to be influenced by the visual language of another material as by the behaviour of a particular glaze or firing process. In the teapot illustrated, some of the characteristics of objects made by a tin smith may be perceived. Keeler has identified those characteristics and treated them, not in a superficial way which would make the pot look as if it were made of tin, but by interpreting their detail at the junctures of base, spout and handle, places where in tin objects there are specific criteria to address. The pot also plays with the notion of making curvilinear shapes from flat sheets, and puts all this grammar of ideas together with an exploration of the process of salt glazing.

Takeshi Yasuda, b.1943

Takeshi Yasuda is a Japanese potter who has moved to work in the West. He trained in an Eastern pottery, and brought with him a passion for the importance of pottery in the way we live our lives. His pots are thrown using soft clay, and he handles the work with strength and fine sensitivity, characteristics that are apparent in the finished result. The plate illustrated on page 29 has been intentionally distorted when freshly thrown, by grasping and lifting the rim.

The distorted rim has had a handle attached, emphasizing this detail. The artist calls this glazed ware 'sancei', meaning 'three-colour', referencing Chinese Tang dynasty pottery. Yasuda epitomizes the potter whose work largely draws its influence from an attitude to making that stems from his own cultural background; he conveys this influence to a worldwide audience by way of international exhibitions of his work. This is a particular phenomenon of the studio pottery movement that has grown in the era of mass communication.

Will Levi Marshall, b.1969

I have chosen Marshall as the potter who best represents the current international nature of learning and exchange of ideas. Marshall studied in both Britain and North America, and has travelled extensively, absorbing ideas as much as influences.

The plate illustrated is an example of Marshall's interest in developing oxidized stoneware glazes. The incorporation of industrial ceramic transfers and gold lustre extend this potter's sense of enquiry beyond the constraints of traditional studio pottery practice. Gratifyingly, it has become increasingly common to

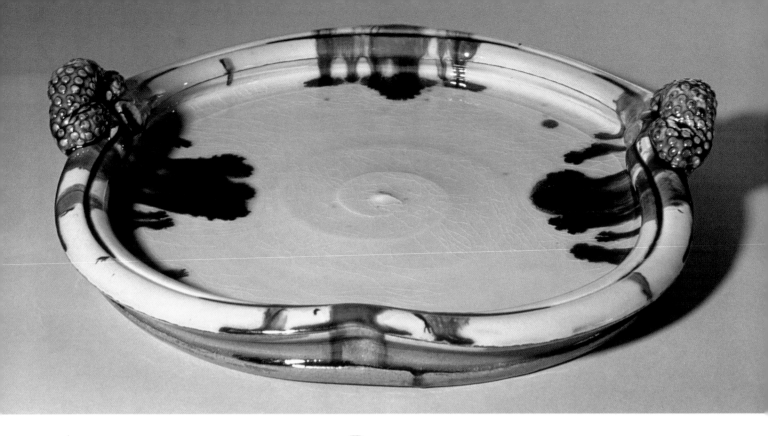

*A*bove. Large plate by Takeshi Yasuda. Width 57cm (22.5in). Oxidized stoneware. 1989.

*B*elow. Dish by Will Levi Marshall. Width 48cm (19in). Oxidized stoneware with enamels and transfer. 1999.

*'K*ings and Queens' by Susan Halls. Height 10cm (4in) (each figure). Thrown and assembled. Salt-fired. 1996

see young potters challenging perceptions of the boundaries of exploration. He makes use of modern computer technology to help him refine and develop glaze recipes which he is keen to share with others. Computer programmes have revolutionized glaze calculation enabling potters to make numerous modifications which previously would have taken hours of longhand mathematics. The use of the internet has encouraged the global exchange of glaze and clay recipes with software helping to translate new recipes using appropriate local raw materials. This information exchange has encouraged the debate of ideas other than purely technical. Marshall is part of that new generation of makers intent on maintaining a passion for the subject, who have a devotion to sharing cross-cultural ideas, and whose work determinedly keeps the movement alive by contributing challenging new pottery that explores the art of throwing.

Susan Halls, b.1966

Susan Halls is one of the most gifted manipulators of clay today. Her work crosses boundaries of process, seeking to explore the intrinsic characteristics of many aspects of making practice, and integrating these characteristics as part of a personal expression. She is a British potter who now lives and works in North America. She often uses throwing as the basis from which to develop ideas; for instance, in 'Kings and Queens' (*see* illustration above) the thrown component parts sometimes required little alteration to give them new meaning – for example as a stole or a cloak.

The use of process by contemporary practitioners is not constrained by any philosophical boundaries that might decree what may be made on the wheel; however, the best work does acknowledge the idea of truth to materials through a deep respect for the characteristics with which materials and process inform work.

2 Throwing, a Language of Expression

Listen again. One Evening at the Close
Of Ramazan, ere the better Moon arose,
In that old Potter's Shop I stood alone
With the clay Population round in Rows.
And, strange to tell, among that Earthen Lot
Some could articulate, while others not:
And suddenly one more impatient cried –
'Who is the Potter, pray, and who the Pot?'

From the *Rubaiyat* of Omar Khayyam,
a twelfth-century Persian poet.

Omar Khayyam understood there was more to pottery than a potter making a pot: rather, it is the result of the potter's creative endeavour on the wheel, and this can communicate in an expressive manner – it may be thought of as an amalgam of the combined influence of maker, materials, process and circumstance. It is this collective expression contained within the object that fascinates potters, driving them to explore subtle nuances within what is undoubtedly a language.

The very act of throwing clay on the wheel inspires many ideas of what to make – but where do ideas come from? Arguably they are born from personal experience, since every impulse we have can be connected to something we have seen or done. It is the nature of design to respond to experience, sometimes very logically when trying to solve a problem, at others in a seemingly haphazard way when responding to an emotion.

Ideas represent the beginning stage of the process of making good pots. Not all will be productive or worthwhile, and there are many reasons for discarding ideas – they may be uninteresting or too difficult to realize; besides, everyone discards more than they use. This selective process is important: it is a way of sifting ideas until one in particular catches the attention and is developed further, the possibility of its becoming a reality explored, and this measured against other ideas to judge its relative merits.

Discovering the language of objects and the means of generating ideas helps us to understand more about pottery, perhaps to gain a deeper appreciation of those inanimate but highly communicative pots.

Drawing

Drawing is an extremely useful tool of communication, since it is far easier to describe ideas

*T*ile by Bernard Leach, with a drawing of a bottle. 10 × 10cm (4 × 4in). Reduced stoneware. c. 1960.

for objects in visual terms than in written language. Drawing is fast, personal and descriptive; it may precede work on the wheel, or accompany it. Drawing can be used to help resolve problems or to clarify mental images, and it is an indispensable means of recording information for future reference. Some potters make drawings of their work during glazing as a means of recording what treatment has been given to a particular pot, or when unpacking the kiln to document the position of a specific pot. These drawings, often described in a dismissive way as thumbnail sketches, are usually very accurate images, in the way that most purposeful drawings are. An example of purposeful drawing is described by Nesrin During, when writing about the French potter Pierre Bayle:

> At most he produces two or three new shapes per year. He usually starts out with a rough idea sketched on a plank in his studio; then comes the work of creating the form, which is his 'search'. He makes variation upon variation, drawing each in his notebook – pages and pages of the same form with annotations on the small changes.

('Quest for Beauty' by Nesrin During. *Ceramics Monthly*, January 2001.)

Some people make drawings or designs of the pots they intend to throw. However, it is unusual to see someone attempting to make an accurately thrown version of a carefully drawn pot. In a well-known film of Bernard Leach we see him taking a selection of fine drawings from his desk and deciding which pot to make. Leach was an exceptional draughtsman, and perfectly capable of reproducing accurately his paper design – but the drawing is a separate creation from the pot, it has its own purpose, which is to clarify an idea that must be responded to in a different manner when wet clay is spinning through the potter's hands.

The drawings of jugs in my sketchbook show some of the ideas that were in my mind at the time. Variations on a theme are described quickly, without worrying about making them accurate designs: it is the spirit of the idea that is being explored. I make drawings such as this during a making session, the drawings neither preceding nor following the work, but accompanying the activity of making and responding to thoughts that need to be recorded. Drawing is simply a useful tool to be used as and when required.

The surface of the large pitcher, made by the author, was brushed with white and iron slips prior to drawing sgraffito decoration with a wooden tool. The emphasis of the decoration spirals upwards, complementing the horizontal throwing lines that make the form appear lively and fresh. The pot has pronounced speckling as it was made from a fire-clay body that contains many particles of iron. Ideas for decorating a pot are readily explored through drawing before making a commitment to any one idea, which will gain permanence.

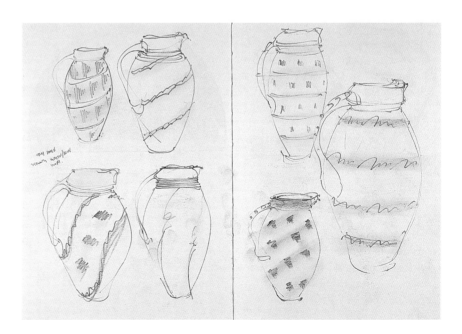

Drawings from the author's sketchbook.

*S*alt-glaze pitcher, by
Alex McErlain. Height
40cm (16in).
Stoneware. 1983.
(Alan Firth)

Learning from the Past

In the twentieth century and to the present day, potters have had easy access to the work of other periods and civilizations from all around the world. In some ways, however, this easy referencing of other pottery is too much of a good thing. The curator and writer Michael Robinson described it as the 'magic wardrobe' of ideas, where potters could 'try on' some of the 'clothes' for suitability. Learning from predecessors has always been a key way to develop understanding. Knowledge of how to throw passes from one person to another; knowledge of form may pass between communities; and knowledge of style has crossed international boundaries through trade routes. But with so much pottery accessible through museum collections, books and exhibitions, it is sometimes difficult to know how to make best use of the abundance of information. When studying objects from other cultures it is vital to find out about the context in which the pot was made in order to gain a real understanding.

Living, as we do, in the age of digital photography, drawing historical pots is perhaps not the best way to make a quick record – but to draw is to look with great intensity, and this sort of close scrutiny is by far the best route to gaining an understanding of someone else's creation. For this reason potters are often found scrutinizing pots in museum collections, and making drawings to record what they see. But it is important to be aware that the past should be studied to deepen knowledge, not just to plunder it for ideas. Good pots will emerge from the influence of other cultures if they are an expression of an individual's own ideas, and not simply facsimiles.

Pots in Archaeology

The history of a civilization is often revealed and better understood through the pottery that is left behind. Archaeologists expect to find evidence of differing societies through pottery shards, primarily because these outlast all other materials. Sometimes this tells them a lot about the society: the pottery may contain traces of the food that was eaten, the spices or medicine or perfumes used. The moratoria shards left behind on Roman sites are evidence of how these bowls were designed for preparing food, since their inside surface is gritty so that food may be more easily ground up. Some shards are impressed with a name of the maker. A large quantity of shards might indicate a production centre, as well as telling us about the everyday life of the people. Those aspects of what a society valued is sometimes depicted in drawings on pottery.

Archaeologists may learn about travel and communication by examining clay bodies (which they refer to as the 'fabric' of the pot) in

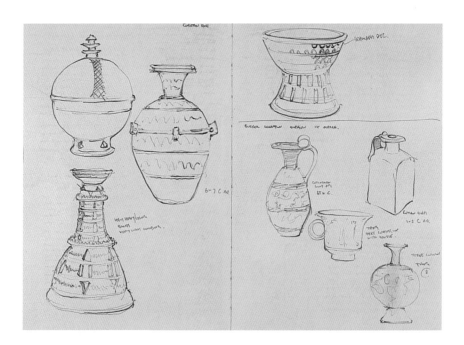

Design studies of historical pots.

order to identify where they came from. Stylistic influences may be tracked across continents providing evidence of travel. The pottery of North America shows clearly the influences from Germany, Britain and France in the shapes and styles the potters adopted; as these became assimilated, eventually a whole new set of characteristics evolved that we identify with nineteenth-century American wares.

Archaeology makes good use of the information contained within a pottery shard: with practice it will be interpreted and understood, and may form the basis of an historical record. The same language is used when pots are made today: thus when we sit on the wheel we hold the potential to make objects with which we will communicate with future generations.

Understanding the Language of Pots

Pots can communicate to us in many ways if we take the trouble to understand their language. Looking, understanding what is seen, and analysing what this tells you, leads to a fuller knowledge and hopefully appreciation of pottery. By making a structured analysis of context, form, content and process it is quite possible to develop an understanding of the language of pots.

- **Context** refers to where and when an object was made – the society in which it was created and subsequently used. Context may change – for example a pot made for storing grain in Cyprus may end up as a garden planter in Britain; this in turn can affect the development of the pot as an export item.
- **Form** describes the shape of an object, its proportional arrangements, its visual and tactile characteristics and its degree of formality or informality.
- **Content** addresses what a pot is about: its purpose may be utilitarian, or as a vehicle for decoration, it may be a political propaganda item, or simply a fun object, as in the case of a puzzle jug.
- **Process** describes the way a pot was made, the materials used, and their influence on both the maker and the object. An understanding of process is central to pottery appreciation as well as pottery making.

'I use local materials insofar as I can for slips and glazes. The materials that you gather and process yourself are impure, they are unrefined, and that gives the glaze a greater character and depth and a certain unpredictability, which I like, and an unrepeatability, which I also like. It makes the pots completely indigenous to the area, the pots are actually part of the place they come from.' Jim Malone, July 1997.

Context, form, content and process are all interrelated within an object, and consequently elements overlap; but use these concepts as headings to make a structured analysis, and this will provide a means of developing deeper knowledge. This approach is illustrated in the following analysis of two pots, one made in the nineteenth century and the other in the twenty-first century.

The English Pancheon

The pancheon is an interesting form to examine when trying to understand the contributing factors that resulted in its particular design. The word 'pancheon' describes a large, straight-sided bowl with a narrow base and a wide rim. This seemingly innocuous pot was once an everyday item, but with a complex set of design factors.

Pancheons were made extensively throughout Britain during the nineteenth century, and came in a range of sizes measured in inches from 12in (30cm) to 24in (60cm) in diameter. They evolved in response to a requirement for vessels for domestic use, and were made in, and supplied to, rural communities with similar domestic activities for which the pot was designed. 'Designed' implies that it appeared in its distinctive format at one moment in time, which was not the case; rather its shape evolved according to the uses required of it. Thus the largest pancheons were used for laundry and are usually described as washing pancheons; smaller ones were used in the bedroom for personal hygiene, and were described in the same way.

As a practical domestic item the pancheon's *form* has some useful physical characteristics. The fat rim is helpful when lifting, particularly if the hands are wet, when a firm grip is

Washing pancheon. Width 60cm (24in). English earthenware. Nineteenth century. (Alex McErlain)

required. The wide surface diameter ensures good access for all those tasks that involve extensive hand movement, for example washing, kneading bread or skimming cream in the dairy. The flat base provides stability, particularly important for a container that often holds liquid. Most pancheons were slipped inside to develop a pale colour, since this is associated with cleanliness; it also enabled the contents to be clearly seen.

The design of the pancheon is also influenced by *process*, that is, the materials and methods used in its making: these are an integral part of the development of the form. The clay is red earthenware, locally dug, and this is significant because it has an inherent plasticity that means the shape will stand up on the wheel without collapsing. It would be very difficult to make such a form with some other clays – for example, porcelain would not readily support a heavy rim on a wide flaring shape. It is because red earthenware has this special plasticity that the potters were able to develop the large, simple forms that we associate with country pottery.

As we have already mentioned, the inside of the pancheon is coated in a white slip so the glaze looks pale in colour. The glaze itself is made of galena and clay, and is yellow in

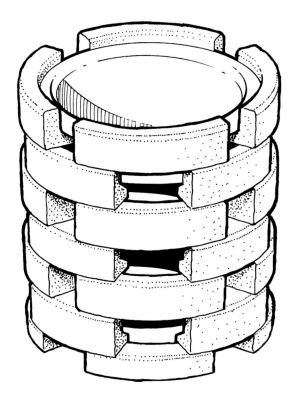

Washing pancheons stacked in pan rings for firing.

colour because of the iron content of the clay: applied over the red clay it will always appear brown, because the clay is a darker colour than the glaze.

Pancheons were fired in stacks using pan rings; this method used the kiln space more efficiently, and also protected the wares during firing.

The walls of the pancheon are straight so that one could be suspended inside another, and the rim is shaped to sit in the pan ring.

The rim also helps with glazing and slipping, operating like the lip of a jug to cut off the flow of liquid and stop it running down the outside of the form. When the pot was glazed the potter would run a finger under the rim to ensure it was clear of glaze.

The design of this pot is therefore a consequence of where it was made, and why and how, and also what it was made from, and for. All these factors contribute to a design that evolved over a period of time and resulted in an object perfectly suited to its manufacture and purpose. This process may be described as 'evolutionary design' as opposed to 'revolutionary design'.

The visual characteristics of the pancheon also relate to the context in which it was made and used. The form looks strong, and has in-

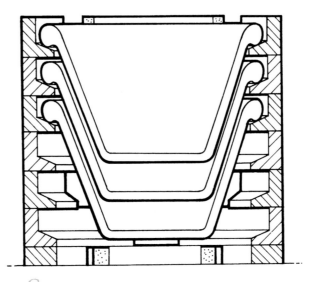

Section drawing of washing pancheons stacked in the kiln.

built strengthening characteristics, such as, for example, the rolled rim. The rural communities used these objects constantly in their daily life, in the kitchen, farmyard and dairy, and so they needed to withstand the occasional knock; inevitably they would eventually break, when a replacement would be needed, thus confirming a demand for continuity of supply. This meant,

Le Bol by Takeshi Yasuda. Height 10cm (4in). Distorted porcelain. 2001.

of course, that the pots had to be made in quantity, which in turn meant that both design and production had to be efficient if they were to be economical to make and sell.

From an aesthetic point of view, the natural warm colours of red clay and yellow glaze harmonized well with the rural environment in which pancheons were used. The throwing emphasized softened contours, the proportions are bold, and the overall feeling is one of confidence in a vessel that seems to say 'Use me'.

A Modern Pot

It is interesting to examine a modern pot in a similar way. The bowl entitled 'Le Bol', made by the contemporary artist potter, Takeshi Yasuda, is a quite different object from the pancheon, and has its own language to read. The relationship of clay to glaze in the case of 'Le Bol' is almost inseparable, and the *content* of the pot deals with the hardness and softness of materials, the translucency of clay and glaze, and the way a sense of movement may be captured in a static object. Made from Limoges porcelain, the

bowl is translucent and in places transparent where the clay is pierced by the impressed tool, the gap filled with glaze.

'Le Bol' celebrates the process of softly thrown porcelain, a clay body that is very demanding to use. The rim is distorted in two places to make an undulating circle, and the wall of the bowl has four sets of three indents, applied in diagonal lines, creating pockets of shadow that emphasize the movement in the form. The pronounced ridge at the base is impressed in four places to echo the undulations of the rim. The thin edge of this ridge turns slightly upwards, generating a linear form that is highlighted by light and shadow, describing a line that echoes the linear movements at the rim.

On the underside the pot has been turned to make a softly contoured foot-ring together with a sharp-edged line at the point where the turning ceased. The foot gently undulates like a soft cushion where four scars remain, a permanent legacy of the firing support; the scars all radiate outwards and are aligned with the four indents in the wall. The numerics are important to this pot, as they are to many other pots with

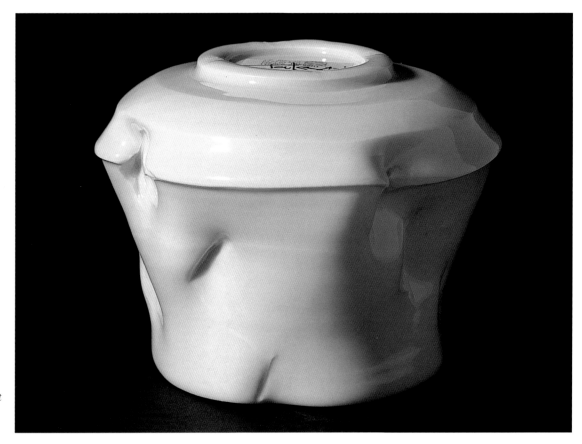

'Le Bol' (foot) by Takeshi Yasuda. Height 10cm (4in). Distorted porcelain. 2001.

deliberate proportional sub-divisions. When fired, porcelain becomes very hard and the body begins to fuse, making it translucent; these characteristics are emphasized in 'Le Bol' through the choice of a clear shiny glaze. Thus the pot looks and feels hard, the movements generated in the form appearing to be still fluid, yet captured as a frozen moment in time.

The stylistic influences on the washing pancheon were entirely local, and the society in which it was made would not have had access to pottery made by other civilizations throughout history. 'Le Bol', however, was made at a time when we are all aware of historical pots, and it is interesting to compare it with those pots that deal with a similar language of expression. This bowl may be related to the fine ding wares made in China during the eleventh century, pots with a remarkable sensitivity to the softness and clarity of form captivated in hard-fired clay. Ding bowls were often delicately incised with foliage patterns, the ones glazed ivory generating interest through the play of light on and through form. The connections with Yasuda's work and Leeds cream ware, made in England during the late eighteenth century, have been remarked upon by some critics, mainly due to the similarities of colour; however, the comparison may be too simplistic, and only of peripheral significance when trying to gain a deeper understanding of this artist's work.

It can be too easy to make direct connections between historical work, which contemporary potters are more than aware of, and the creative endeavours of an individual. Whilst some potters draw inspiration directly from historical sources, the most creative artists will assimilate knowledge from many sources whilst developing their own particular creative language of expression.

Examining the context of the pot is fundamental to developing a fuller understanding of its implications. 'Le Bol' is made by an artist who has added his signature to a label on the base, and it exists within the studio pottery movement where individual artists express themselves through the medium of clay. The pot is not specifically designed for use, although it may be used; the artist has in fact built himself a reputation for making pottery for use with food, sensual forms that add to the pleasure of a meal. It is a very tactile pot, which helps in appreciating the subtle inter-relationships of the movements in form. This pot says 'touch me' rather than 'use me', although perhaps the act of touching is actually a use, bringing together visual and tactile senses to gain pleasure.

By analysing pottery in this way a fuller appreciation of the object may be gained, and the argument that the pot should 'speak for itself' is upheld; through learning how to read the language its 'voice' may be more clearly heard.

Designing for Use

Purposeful design is synonymous with many thrown pots. The process of making thrown pottery is so fast that historically there was little competition from other materials when it came to supplying the utilitarian needs of a community. The speed of manufacture and the ability to modify designs drove the evolutionary development of many basic pottery forms such as the jug or teapot. Within the basic configurations many variations exist, and this continues to attract potters into making their own recognizable repertoire of forms. Pots designed for use will normally sell quickly if they are attractive to the consumer, consequently the production of a whole range of utilitarian ware will help the potter to survive financially, and may even subsidize less commercial endeavours.

The most significant factor in designing pots for use is practicality. If a teapot does not pour, or a casserole cannot survive the oven, then however good it looks, it will be useless. A pot must function well to be successful, but that function must also embrace giving pleasure to the user. The process of design, which begins with the potter, the materials and the methods, is made complete by the person who uses the pot. There is a communication between maker, object and user that is quietly significant, and it is this communication that continues to drive contemporary potters to design and make pots for use. The most favourable compliment must surely be: 'I do enjoy using your pots!'

Prototypes

Designing functional pottery normally involves developing prototypes, taking the idea from the wheel, through the kiln and into the kitchen to see how the object works in practice before returning to the wheel to make modifications.

Tea set by Jim Malone. Reduced stoneware. 1978. The need to develop designs for differing items that interrelate is a major challenge for the potter. Malone's tea set is visually linked not only by sympathetic form, but by the glaze and decoration.

Prototyping domestic ware intended for regular production may involve taking into consideration the economics of the production process. A good example of this may be seen in the design of a simple bowl for eating cereal, a pot in the repertoire of many studios. It is normally produced in fairly large quantities, so an important consideration is modifying the design to fit economically in the kiln setting. If the pots are unglazed on the rim they can be stacked in the firing, rim to rim and foot to foot, perhaps three or four bowls high. In this way a regular layer of pots may be included in every firing, the diameter of the bowl dictating how many fit on a kiln shelf and what may be designed to fit between them. By developing a design that is compatible with these factors the unit cost of production will be minimized, and the studio may be made more economically viable.

Prototypes by Alex McErlain. Height 10cm (4in). Reduced stoneware. 1997.

Some potters call pots of this type their 'bread-and-butter wares' as they provide regular income and help offset some of the costs associated with making more time-consuming projects. The challenge of design for use is an exciting one for the potter; within its parameters lie the opportunity for invention, self-expression and communication, with a seemingly inexhaustible set of solutions.

Understanding Form

The word 'form' is constantly used when describing pottery, and seems to be central to many interpretations of what constitutes a good pot. In fact 'form' simply describes the shape and arrangement of parts of an object, but when used in conjunction with an adjective such as 'strong', 'subtle', 'bold', 'sensual' or 'weak', its intention is to convey something more than a simple arrangement of parts. Potters often evaluate the success of a pot by initially commenting on its form. This is because the form of a pot is seen as central to the success of its other aspects: therefore even if a pot has a most beautiful glaze, if it is on a poor form it will always be considered a poor pot. The painter Patrick Heron, when writing about pottery, described form in relation to 'the human figure, where the structural form is below the surface of the flesh – the bone is under the muscle' (*The Changing Forms of Art*, 1955).

The form of a thrown pot is principally established during throwing; it may be modified by turning, but if there is weakness in the initial thrown form, this will not be disguised by turning. Form must encompass many aspects of the art of throwing – proportion, function, finish, the dynamics of a pot – and hold these aspects together in a way that is visually satisfying.

Consider the coffee jug made by Mike Dodd, a simple pot that relies heavily on form for its visual characteristics. The form appears extremely decisive, the result of having been handled in a bold manner. The initial thrown form consists of two curved shapes, the convex form of the belly and the concave form of the neck. The meeting point of the curves is marked by a deeply cut line that has filled with glaze. The convex curve has been subdivided with two incised lines about a third of the way up the

Coffee jug by Mike Dodd. Height 16cm (6½in). Reduced stoneware. The sunken lid is ideal for a coffee jug as it uses the low centre of gravity to counteract the action of pouring from a tall proportioned form.

curve, and the ratio of the concave section to the convex section is about one third to two thirds. These proportional divisions correspond to golden section divisions. Both curves follow one continuous line, with the centre of the curves being the widest and narrowest part respectively. Six bulbous panels have been created by pressing a tool into the soft clay, leaving a pronounced mark at each end of the vertical line. The rim of the pot is thickened in a proportion that relates to the lines created by incision at the juncture of the two curves.

When the pot was being thrown Dodd must have taken into consideration the nature and behaviour of the glaze that would cover its surface. The glaze is composed principally of wood ash, and although its behaviour in the firing is somewhat erratic, nonetheless it is in ways that may be anticipated. Thus the glaze will flow at high temperature, moving across surfaces, creating dark glassy pools where it gathers thickly, and paler broken colours where it has thinned. The underlying form of this pot anticipates this behaviour and works to exploit it to the full. The dynamic created by the bulbous panels has been further developed with the movements created in the handle. The form of the handle – which must still pay heed to function, in that it must accommodate a bunch of fingers, all the while keeping them well away from the surface of the hot container – is fluid in its movements, creating a surface that would respond to the character of glaze. The additions of beak-shaped spout and knob are both curvilinear in form, completing the composition in a bold but sympathetic manner.

The pot is therefore more than the sum of its parts, but by analysing its essential elements it has been possible to understand how the artist composed this essay in curvilinear form with such success.

In the words of Jim Malone: 'I plan what I am going to make . . . It doesn't work for me if I approach the wheel in a woolly state of mind. I need to know clearly and exactly what I am intending to do.'

Good form is a consequence of planned action that takes into account the materials and processes; action that may be developed slowly or with quick gestural movements, and which recognizes the underlying dynamics of a composition. Above all, there must be vitality encapsulated in the design through making. Weakness in form is often a consequence of indecision, or a lack of sensitivity to proportion, process and materials. The clumsy efforts of a beginner will often produce a pot that is quite poor in form because of the lack of control – although even as skill is acquired, the potter must be aware that progress in making skills will not automatically result in pottery with good form. It helps to study form, to make comparisons, and to seek opinions about form until understanding deepens and confidence develops.

The Studio

The environment in which pots are created is of fundamental importance: the potter must be able to concentrate in a comfortable situation, with tools and materials near to hand, together with a sympathetic ambience to suit the individual. The primary aim should be to make the circumstances conducive to the production of good work. The characteristics of a studio can be inspirational, the mood determined by the materials and sounds that prevail. Bernard Leach made reference to this in *A Potter's Book*, a work that influenced the whole development of post-war studio pottery:

An individual potter's workshop means more to him than a mere setting where the routine of production can conveniently go on. Here

*P*atrick Sargent in his workshop. Switzerland 1998. (Marcus Rusch)

he has to seek and weigh new ideas, comparing them and his finished work with the standards of the past and the needs of an unborn future.

It is interesting to compare the studios and workshops of different potters. The very name that the potter gives to the place of work carries its own connotations; thus some of the most creative individuals will insist on it being called a 'workshop', as that is where the creative work is carried out. Does the studio therefore belong more to the artist, and the workshop to the craftsman?

Although the surroundings in which pots are made may vary hugely from one studio to another, one common factor is a source of good lighting. Without good light it is difficult to see form clearly, which in turn will impair the ability to make. Some potters like to have the wheel facing a window to take advantage of natural light, but whilst the view from the window may be helpful to some, others consider it to be a source of distraction that will interrupt the intense concentration they put into their work. Those orderly studios where the wheel faces a blank wall with a solitary electric light

> The main work is not to make pots, but to allow them to develop and grow, to be alive, and to communicate warmth and life in that uncannily direct and undemanding way that true and naked work can, vulnerable as it is.
> (Richard Batterham)

are like a shrine, where nothing is allowed to interrupt concentration. And whilst background noise is important for some potters, music or the radio playing can either help concentration, or disturb it. The common factor is concentration: if this is interrupted through distractions, then the pots will suffer.

Skill

A number of potters have described skill as a dangerous asset that must be treated with caution. Skill is necessary if a potter wishes to be able to manipulate clay on the wheel without struggling, and it is acquired and maintained through practice. If a potter is not skilful enough it will normally show clearly in his work, and this may be in obvious ways – for example the pot may be too heavy for its scale,

or it may be overtly wobbly, in a manner which is obviously not intentional.

Having the skill to manipulate clay exactly how you want is a wonderful sensation – but there must be more to a good pot than skill alone, and those who commented on the dangers of skill were referring to this possibility. Some pots positively celebrate skill, displaying with panache a series of characteristics that are known to be difficult to achieve; and in a really good pot the maker's concern for form and expression will be an integral part of its creation – Cardew described it as 'technique and inspiration being as one'. There are also pots that appear to disregard skill altogether; in practice, however, they are usually the ones that require the most skill to make.

Skill cannot be avoided, but it is best acquired over time, and should be used with care, avoiding slickness.

Sensitivity

Along with skill, the potter must acquire sensitivity in all aspects of design and manufacture if his pots are to become really good. Sensitivity in making means understanding and respecting the materials, working positively with their characteristics, and not forcing them to do

*T*eapot by Sarah Walton. Salt-glaze stoneware, 1982. The very thin layer of salt glaze on this pot highlights the skill and sensitivity that went into the making. (Margaret Weller)

Charger by Michael Casson. Width 48cm (19in). Wood-fired stoneware, 1987. The pot has only been glazed on the rim, the rest being affected by the wood firing that produced rich colours from the very dark clay body coated with white slip.

things inappropriate to their nature. Thus when throwing and turning, the clay should be in the optimum condition for the task in hand. For instance, trying to throw clay that is too stiff will not produce a sensitive result because what you are trying to achieve will be a struggle right from the outset. The potter should aim to make clean, positive movements when working; being decisive and carrying out tasks with confidence all contribute to sensitivity.

Sensitivity can be engendered by thinking carefully about every aspect of making, not taking anything for granted, and by paying great attention to detail.

Uniformity

Throwing a group of pots to the same size and shape is relatively easy, with practice; however, they will not be exactly uniform, as hand

forming, and the nuances this implies, is an implicit part of the process. Machine technology does make exact uniformity possible, for example through the use of a jigger jolley machine, a close relative of throwing; but the whole point of making by hand is to celebrate the creation of a form that reflects the individual as well as the process. This is certainly the rationale for studio pottery, but it was also an implicit part of pre-twentieth-century pottery, which valued those characteristics of purposeful work.

When a small workshop is engaged in producing pots to the same design, the individuals working together will be able to recognize each others work instantly, as the nuances within each form are part of the expression of an individual, their own personal language. A really sensitive pottery workshop will recognize this, and accept that an individual's interpretation of an idea is more acceptable than rigorous standardization. Thrown pottery that strives too hard to achieve uniformity will always run the risk of being dull and lifeless. This is not to say that pots cannot be made with accuracy without losing vitality, but rather that the emphasis of intention should be on each pot achieving the best possible vitality whilst being accurately proportioned.

Precision

The wheel may be used as a precision instrument, and some potters take great pleasure in exploring this quality. The ancient Greeks led the way in precision throwing, and some contemporary potters are also attracted by this characteristic. The work of Felicity Aylieff makes use of the wheel to develop individual forms that are precisely finished and polished, with close attention to detail. Those characteristics are made possible by selecting an appropriate clay body and working the clay when it is in precisely the right condition for the process in hand. The work has associations with engine-turned pottery produced in Staffordshire during the 1760s.

The wheel enables clay to be rapidly burnished, and this produces a dense surface that allows the characteristics of the body composition to be seen in detail. Bodies used for precision throwing are usually selected for their fired characteristics as well as the ability to respond

to the process. Thus redware bodies are frequently used for precision throwing as they are particularly responsive to detailed cutting, and reveal subtle colours when fired without glaze. Grogged clays will not lend themselves to the finest 'engine' turning, but may reveal interesting characteristics when burnished, as the grog becomes compressed into the plastic clay.

An interesting side effect of heavily burnished thrown pottery is the revelation after firing of faint throwing lines, a result of activating clay 'memory'.

The Kiln and its Influence on Design

The potter's kiln plays an important role in the development of ideas; for instance, it may be intended for a specific firing temperature or atmosphere, which to some extent dictates what may be attempted. The fuel a kiln burns also has an effect on clays and glazes. Potters using coal-fired kilns, for example, often protected the ware in saggers, which in turn brought some restrictions to the scale and shape of the pots.

In Japan, pots that show evidence of a prolonged firing with wood have long been prized, and have been very influential on the studio pottery movement worldwide. Their natural

Asymmetric vessels by Felicity Aylieff. Height 25cm (10in). Thrown and constructed porcelain. (Felicity Aylieff)

Small bottle, coke-fired and encrusted with a deposit from the burning fuel.

fired in the controlled surroundings of an electric kiln must make provision for the glaze to run, and be stopped with precision in order to allow the crystal growth to be controlled. It is important to recognize that design must take into account the inevitable contribution that the kiln will make to the creative output.

Drawing on the Wheel

The wheel offers the opportunity to explore ideas with immediacy: this may be described as drawing in three dimensions, exploring one idea after another, making adjustments and modifications each time until a group of ideas is assembled. Some potters revel in this process, their pots appearing to be the result of an outpouring of ideas. The process is usually refined

feel and asymmetric form are in stark contrast to many Western pots. Pots intended for long firings in an anagama kiln must not only take into account the deposit of ash and the extremes of temperature, but must also make a contribution to guiding the passage of flame around a cross-draught chamber.

In the illustration of Patrick Sargent's kiln, the pots can be seen laid on their sides dripping with ash glaze. The setting was deliberate, anticipating and deflecting the flame passage and consequent ash deposition, which in effect contributed to the design of the pot. Sargent wrote about the creative potential of wood firing: his argument was that creative acts are not concluded the moment pots are set in the kiln, but that by working in partnership with the kiln, further creative development is possible.

This is a dramatic example of the role the kiln may play in design, although it is not unique. Raku firings present specific demands in relation to lifting and removing hot pots; salt and soda kilns demand design features to deal with the fact that everything becomes glazed during the firing; and crystalline glazed wares

Patrick Sargent's kiln after firing. Switzerland, 1998. (Marcus Rusch)

'The best pots, the most successful, incorporate a balance of form, weight, colour, surface qualities and a deposit of ash which, when successfully brought together, form a unity.' Patrick Sargent.

through editing, discarding and retaining pots in equal measure.

The disadvantages of drawing on the wheel appear when dealing with more complex forms that are composite in nature. Drawing on the wheel may be used as a prototyping design methodology, or as a means of developing throwing, which stresses gestural movement, those swiftly made marks that leave behind the evidence of their making.

The bowl made by Patrick Sargent is a good example of gestural throwing. Sargent made pots like these in small batches, throwing fairly quickly and using the falling momentum of a heavy flywheel that demanded decisive and economic hand movements. The interior of the bowl undulates with the motion of the fingers, and has been coated with a thick layer of white slip. This continues the gestural theme, with the brushmarks swirling around the surface providing a background for the colours developed in

the kiln. A rounded tool has been pushed into the wall of the bowl to make ten indents, left slightly rough to give tactile interest, and to punctuate the movements of the glaze.

Hamada's approach to throwing seems to encapsulate the idea of drawing on the wheel. Janet Leach described seeing Hamada at work:

Watching Mr Hamada throw, it is obvious that he is conscious of the nature of the material he is using – clay – and of the form he has in mind. There are no repressions or regulations governing accuracy or precision relating to the machine. He is striving for the spirit of the form in clay, and his working method is always as we observed on his tour in America: the pot comes up, and at the first spontaneous burst of life he stops working it. It may not be quite smooth, even or centred, but these factors become secondary, and he does not sacrifice spontaneous vitality of form to a mechanical slickness and perfection. (Shoji Hamada, Master Potter)

Drawing on the Pot

The pot as a vehicle for decoration is commonplace throughout ceramic history. Wheel-made

Bowl by Patrick Sargent. Width 15cm (6in), height 12cm (5in). Anagama fired stoneware.

pots, especially plates and large jars with a smooth, uninterrupted surface, invite decorative treatment. In the pot made by Josie Walter, form and decoration integrate well.

The rim of the bowl frames the fish drawing, and the steep-sided interior enables the drawing to suggest movement around the bowl as though the fish were swimming. The bowl is made from red clay, and is covered in coarsely brushed white slip: this reveals parts of the red body, and provides a background for the drawing to work within. When the pot was being made, the decorative treatment was anticipated and so the design took into account the methods that would be used to make the drawing.

The most successfully decorated pots always integrate the surface decoration with form. The incantation bowls made in Mesopotamia in about the fourth century BC take the idea of drawing on the pot into a situation where the inscription invites the reader to hold the pot whilst reading the incantation, thus integrating drawing and form in a very intimate way.

Drawing with the Clay

Thrown forms may be used as components to build figurative work. The artist Susan Halls sometimes makes a work by manipulating thrown elements, developing animal forms that use the characteristics of the throwing process in an unusual format. The method is perhaps best described as 'drawing with the clay'.

In the photograph opposite, the throwing lines in the horse's neck become rippling flesh, and this appears to emphasize the muscular nature of the beast, taut skin enveloping the thrown nose. The work is neither a portrait of a horse nor a composition in throwing, but something that makes us look at the characteristics we recognize in both an animal and in the language of throwing.

The manipulation of spinning clay on the wheel promotes the feeling of physical form almost as if the hands were holding a limb, feeling its shape and modifying its form. Halls

Rider 1, by Sue Halls. Height 18cm (7in). Thrown and assembled. Raku with colloidal slip, 1995. (S. Halls)

'Put Me Nightie
Straight When You've
Done' by Neil
Brownsword. Height
35cm (14in), width
38cm (15in).
Earthenware, 1997.

enjoys the speed with which animal parts may be formulated and the subtle surfaces brought about by handling soft wet clay.

Neil Brownsword also uses throwing when developing his unusual work. The innate characteristics of swiftly thrown modules are used to suggest completely different human elements. We are made aware of the anthropomorphic nature of thrown pots in a surprising way. A tiny thrown bowl is squeezed to give the appearance of an ear, a twisted cylinder becomes a stretched neck. The surface of Brownsword's work is usually covered in shiny glaze, evoking the glistening characteristics of wet clay when first being thrown.

Halls and Brownsword are just two examples of contemporary practitioners who explore the use of the wheel to compose new forms by drawing.

There are many historical examples of thrown component parts being used to make figurative work. Drawing with clay on the wheel in a playful manner is something that harks back to our first experiences of throwing, when even the most wobbly of achievements is mesmerizing in its ability to capture those characteristics that we associate with the art of throwing.

3 Learning and Dreaming

'The training of a potter is a process limited only by the span of his life.'

Michael Cardew, Pioneer Pottery.

Learning the Art of Throwing

Learning is closely related to dreaming – trying to tackle the seemingly impossible in order to realize an ambition or a dream. Little is documented historically about the means by which potters learned their craft. There are significant differences in production levels between the pottery produced to serve a local community, and that to serve a court or an empire. The status of a potter whose work may have been seasonal – such as those mediaeval English potters – was probably fairly low. It is safe to assume that small-scale potteries passed on skills and knowledge from one person to another, perhaps family members, so the acquisition of skill was probably born out of need, rather than desire. In some civilizations such as ancient Greece, the Roman Empire and the Song dynasty in China, the prodigious output of wares with the finest quality of workmanship must have been supported by specialized systems of learning.

Rural Potteries

There is some historical documentation that tells us how potters learned their trade in rural societies during the eighteenth and nineteenth centuries: here, learning to make pots was achieved by becoming an apprentice. An apprenticeship could last between five and eight years, and generally began when the person was fourteen years old. Pottery workers were mostly men, and so normally boys were taken on as apprentices; and it was considered important for these youngsters to be involved in all aspects of the work, from making clay to glazing and firing. Initially, throwing would be learnt through observation whilst making up balls of clay and lifting off finished pots from the thrower's wheel. In those potteries that used a hand-turned wheel, the apprentice would learn by working in conjunction with the

Handled bottle. Made in France. Height 23cm (9in). Stoneware.

thrower. And when he was ready to learn to throw, he would begin with a small, simple form and develop skill through repetition. As his skills advanced, so the more complex forms were introduced, until all the shapes and sizes of pot made by the workshop were within his capabilities.

This method of training flourished until the twentieth century. Skilled throwers might become itinerant workers, moving around to where the demand existed. In some countries, for example Germany, the growth in demand for stoneware pottery led to the establishment of workshops in production centres that specialized in thrown ware employing skilled workers.

Industrial Throwing

The development of factories in eighteenth-century England to make large quantities of pottery brought about a change in the way an individual was trained. The way in which the factory labour force was divided meant that to be a thrower was a specialized job. An apprentice thrower might learn to make a few shapes in quantity at high speed, but the pots would be turned on a lathe by another operator, and the ware was normally turned all over the outside of the pot, to eliminate throwing characteristics in

an attempt to ensure uniformity. So although throwing was an efficient method of production for factories, it was heavily reliant on the skill of an individual, and eventually slip casting came to dominate production methods.

Some factories began to employ artists and designers to produce special items known as 'art pottery', in which the artist designed a shape for a thrower to make up. This separation of the creative power from the object maker resulted in pots that are distinctive by their lack of those characteristics that derive from the process of manufacture. The perception of the artist or designer as a person who did not actually make the work provoked a counter movement, which eventually led to what is now known as studio pottery.

Early Studio Potters

Bernard Leach and other early studio potters learned by seeking out someone to teach them. Thus Leach learned with a Japanese master, and in turn taught Michael Cardew and many others. The system of workshop training developed by studio potters was refined as workshops grew in number and production expanded. Leach established a range of items that he termed 'standard ware', and this enabled him to employ students who could train in the

Thrown teapot made at the Wedgwood factory. Height 17cm (6.7in).

workshop, learning to make the range of pots and absorbing philosophical ideas at the same time. Soon other potteries adopted this system. Typically a team would be engaged in the regular production of a range of eighty items of useful pottery; frequently there would be six in a team: the pottery owner, three established workers, and two students – in this way a team might change some personnel, yet still be able to make the standard range of items.

Typically a student would stay for two or three years, long enough to become fluent in workshop practices before leaving to establish another workshop that in turn might train others. This system flourished for half a century until the demand for large quantities of standard wares declined in the late twentieth century; this led to a situation where most studio potters now work alone.

Workshop Training

Life as a student training in a professional workshop requires discipline, commitment and perseverance. The workshop atmosphere is organized, and work is undertaken in a regular cycle that usually relates to the number of times the kiln is fired in a year. To begin with a new student would usually be given a few basic tasks that involved working alongside or assisting one of the other workers in order to grasp the rhythm of the working cycle – although over time he would be expected to become involved with all aspects of workshop practice. The first big surprise for most newcomers to a working pottery is how little time is devoted to throwing pots. In a workshop that employs a team of six working to a weekly firing it is usual for all the throwing to be done in two days, the remainder of the time being taken up with clay and glaze preparation, glazing, kiln setting and unloading, organization and despatch of the pottery orders, and general workshop maintenance.

The week's throwing would be organized such that lists were made for each potter. A student would usually be started off making one of the simpler forms such as a small bowl, then progressively other shapes would be introduced that encouraged a logical development to his acquisition of skill and fluency. Thus small bowls might be followed by larger ones, then handled bowls and lidded pots; straightforward beakers would lead to handled beakers, jugs,

coffee jugs and other composite forms. Flatware might begin with small plates, leading to a baking dish, then an oval dish and thence to a casserole. It would normally take quite a long period to develop this repertoire of shapes, as the workshop would not be able to accommodate too many changes at one time; as one potter handed over the production of one particular form to another, so the form contributed by each team member to the range would change, right down the line.

I experienced this system at Winchcombe Pottery in Gloucestershire during the early 1970s, and it convinced me that there was no better way to learn about the intricacies of the art of throwing. However, during the latter years of the twentieth century there was a decline in the number of workshops that could accommodate a team of potters, and so it became more difficult to secure a position to train in these circumstances. In addition, the number of trainees to a workshop is very small, and so a demand grew for special workshops devoted to training new potters.

Decanter made at Winchcombe pottery by Alex McErlain. Height 28cm (11in). Reduced stoneware, 1973. This decanter was designed as a production prototype during the three years the author spent studying at Winchcombe.

Training Workshops

Since the late twentieth century a number of special pottery training workshops have been established, though with varying degrees of success. This is largely because the intention to develop a team comprising mostly of trainees raises the problem of how to make the enterprise economically viable, given that the workforce is largely unskilled. Some training workshops received financial support from government organizations, on the basis that such an investment is worthwhile for the long-term economy of a country.

Workshop trainees may receive a one-year intensive training intended to equip them with the necessary capabilities to make them employable. This methodology seems to work well in countries that have a good tourism industry supporting a number of small production potteries. Other training workshops have tried to develop a production range that will sell in sufficient quantity to support the enterprise; however, by its very nature this demands a team whose membership is of longer term in order to maintain a level of quality and consistency.

The principal difference between the training workshop and a university or college experience is that in the former, the student learns to make work in quantity to a set design, a proposition that is not tenable within an educational environment.

The Wheel in Education

Teaching and learning are two interrelated but quite differing matters. In order to be able to teach well it is vital that the teacher understands that others learn in a variety of ways. The student must appreciate that in order to learn about a subject fully, it is important to acknowledge the many differing approaches to teaching. There are many aspects to study within the subject of the art of throwing, ranging from understanding the relationship of materials, process and expression, to the acquisition of skill. All may be learnt and taught with varying degrees of success, depending to a large extent on the responsiveness of an individual.

The manual skills required for throwing have historically been learnt by passing on knowledge from one individual to another, sometimes via an apprenticeship system. This system of teaching and learning is proven to work well, as we have seen, and until the twentieth century provided the most appropriate means through which skill was acquired.

In the twentieth century many social changes took place, which resulted in there being a number of countries where the art of throwing was no longer practised on any great scale. The development of educational systems, particularly in Britain and America, saw the emergence of specialist schools of art where the creation of wheel-made pottery was included on the curriculum. In the latter part of the twentieth century, the means by which the majority of studio potters initially learned to throw pots was within an art college environment. Some specialist art schools sought to emulate the traditional workshop environment, inviting practitioners to visit and teach the skills required for throwing regular quantities of pottery in an attempt to support those who wished to establish their own workshops or studios. Inevitably, however, the hothouse art college environment, where dreaming is considered an important part of learning, encouraged a greater interest in developing ideas over the acquisition of basic skill, and this led to concerns being expressed in recent years about the perceived decline in the practical abilities of new practitioners. The whole period from 1960 to the present day produced some eminent potters, who would not have discovered the art of throwing were it not for the art school system.

A mixture of art school education followed by workshop training would seem to be the ideal. It remains to be seen what the future holds for those who wish to be taught the basic skills to enable them to learn about the art of throwing.

Studying the Art of Throwing

What to Study

With such a complex subject it is sometimes difficult to know where to begin when embarking on a learning curve – which is daunting, to say the least. The basic skills required to make pots must not be studied in isolation from other important aspects such as form, context and materials; and the study of *why* people make pots is central to developing a personal language of expression. That language may be articulated through making, or writing, or curating; though the quality of these kinds of activities will be dictated to some extent by the depth of knowledge that has been acquired about the subject. Thus a maker who understands these issues will be aware of the importance of making work that is communicative of ideas. A writer who understands about materials and process will be able to make informed observations and deductions about pottery. And a curator who has an understanding of how and why a pot was made will be more sensitive to developing exhibitions that help communication between maker and audience.

'You are interested in pottery; do you know what that means? Do you know that to have the whole world's pottery to look at is like having the whole world's food to eat? Can you digest it? Can you find a way of judging what is a good pot, whether it is made in twelfth-century China, in Persia or Greece, in Europe or by American Indians? How can you come to say with conviction to other people (and yourself), "That is a good pot"? Are you prepared for that? It means a whole life's work, and it means that you must care about it tremendously.' Bernard Leach, *The Potter's Challenge*, 1976.

The subject of pottery is complex and extensive; a lifetime's commitment will be needed to allow enough time for gradual absorption of knowledge and ideas. The study is immensely rewarding, but where to begin?

Watching pots being made must be a priority: there are many opportunities to do this, and it will provide the best introduction to understanding the complexities of what essentially is a very simple and natural process.

Handling pots is vital: through this tactile experience so much may be learnt about the nature of an object. Pots have been made by a human being who imparts a personal identity to the object. The maker would have regarded the sense of touch as a central aspect to his understanding of what was made; so if one is studying a pot, then it would be logical that by handling it you will get some of the same

understanding that the maker had. Watch a potter handling someone else's pot: normally the first thing he will do is invert the pot to examine the foot-ring. Potters are not usually looking for a mark or seal, because if the pot is a good one it will have the maker's signature written all over it in the visual language that it conveys. However, by examining the foot, a potter can read most closely those signs that reveal for example, what the clay body was, how the pot was fired and the degree of sensitivity that the potter's hands gave to the most exposed part. The foot is where the pot is naked standing in the kiln, the part that comes into contact with a shelf or surface without adhering to it.

Using pots forces an intimate understanding of their nature. There is no quicker way to reveal the inadequacies of a poor pot than by using it.

Talking to others about pots will force you to think about ideas, values and making your own judgments.

Reading about pots will broaden and bring greater depth to your knowledge, as will *studying pots* in museums.

Where to Study

It is easy to find situations in which to watch pots being made. Some potters allow visitors to see the work being made on a daily basis, whilst others occasionally open their studios. Public demonstrations at festivals or events bring the opportunity to watch many different potters at work. This is extremely useful as a means of making comparisons, and of discussing ideas directly with the maker; although it must be borne in mind that any public demonstration is an unnatural situation for the maker, when the temptation to play safe or to show a few cheap tricks is fairly high when the prime motivation is to provide entertainment. In-depth demonstrations are sometimes put on for special potters' groups, guilds or societies. These events are much closer to the intimacy of the studio, and are primarily about education and communication, rather than entertainment.

Shops and galleries devoted to selling ceramics provide the opportunity to see a range of work, and a chance to meet other like-minded individuals. The opportunity to handle pots is easily found in places that are trying to sell

them. Whenever you may be contemplating making a purchase, take the opportunity to handle and inspect twenty or so pots, because in the process you will deepen your knowledge each time you do so. Purchasing pots allows you to use them daily – although beware, because it can become addictive!

A number of restaurants serve food in hand-made pots, thus providing the opportunity to use without purchasing. Museums sometimes run handling sessions for small groups, when pieces will be brought out from the display cases for handling and discussion; this is frequently the only way that some people will ever be able to handle historic work. An auction provides a specialized opportunity to study pots, and is normally preceded by viewing days when work may be inspected. Pots that come to auction are sometimes never seen in any other public domain, and for those wishing to broaden their knowledge, the opportunity is one not to be missed.

One of the best situations for discussing pots with others is at the opening of an exhibition, where potters, collectors and supporters gather for a couple of hours, discussion usually revolving around the work on show. In such a situation the maker expects to spend time answering questions and discussing the relative merits of his work. Exhibitions in museums may bring together academics, researchers, curators, writers and makers. Furthermore the opportunity to learn from an exhibition is sometimes enhanced by staged events such as seminars, lectures or demonstrations.

Large, specialist collections of ceramic books exist mostly in academic institutions. Some public libraries have a good selection of ceramic books to study, but if you want access to a few hundred books, then it is probably necessary to enquire about access to an academic institution; this may mean enrolling on a short course.

How to Study

Undoubtedly the best way to learn practically about the art of throwing is to get a good teacher. There are many opportunities to study throwing at all levels. Short courses run by artist potters provide individual tuition to a small number of pupils. Academic institutions offer a wide range of courses, both full and part time. If you are fortunate, you may find a potter willing to employ you as a student. There are many differing approaches taken to learning to make pottery, and it is helpful to watch several different potters throwing, because recognition of the differences makes one more closely aware of the intricacies of the process. Always explore differing ways of doing things for yourself: eventually an approach that is right for *you* will emerge.

There are some excellent seminal texts that every potter should read. The most notable is *A Potter's Book*, written by Bernard Leach, and published in 1940; it has never been out of print, and has influenced the lives of many potters to the extent that it has been called 'the potter's bible'. *A Potter's Book* contains chapters on various aspects of making, with sound advice on all subjects, but it has become renowned for two chapters, one that discusses standards, and the other the working life in the pottery.

Pottery in the Making, edited by Ian Freestone and David Gaimster, should also be on every potter's reading list. It deals with world ceramic traditions, and brings together social, technological and creative insights into the story of the development of pottery. *Ten Thousand Years of Pottery*, by Emmanuel Cooper, is an accessible book with which to begin studying the ceramic work of many civilizations. *The Potter's Dictionary of Materials and Techniques* by Frank and Janet Hamer provides an indispensable reference book, particularly useful for troubleshooting.

The wide range of contemporary magazines devoted to ceramics – such as *Ceramic Review* (UK), *Ceramics Monthly* (USA), *The Studio Potter* (USA) and *Ceramics, Art and Perception* (Australia) all provide good access to current work and the places to see new work.

It is important to recognize that studying the art of throwing will be a progressive learning process, becoming involved in those aspects of making, researching, reading, handling and debating, a body of knowledge and experience that over time will grow, and progressively support a deeper understanding.

Associations

The ceramic world is rich in organizations that support the interests of all who may become involved in pottery: makers, collectors, students, curators and writers, all benefit from the open access that is provided. There are numerous pottery societies and associations around

OPPOSITE:

Coffee jug, by Jim Malone. Height 16cm (6in). Ash-glazed stoneware, 1982.

Ray Finch throwing bowls. Winchcombe Pottery has provided experience for many students in its long history.

the world: some have become renowned for their ambition to reach an international audience, whilst others do sterling work in support of a geographically united group. The Craft Potters Association of Great Britain (CPA) and The National Council on Education for the Ceramic Arts (NCECA) are two long-standing organizations that have promoted access to the subject through organizing events and publishing information. There have been conferences devoted to the wheel, to firing, to exchanging ideas and to a multitude of other subjects. Through attendance at a conference, that vital element of communication is made possible: sharing thoughts, debating ideas and seeing others dealing with the same areas of concern provides support to an individual in ways that are otherwise difficult to achieve.

Collecting

Many potters have small collections of work that they admire that were bought to study and enjoy. The purchase of ceramics completes a creative link that began with an individual devel-

'. . . I really do not know any employment of money more productive of an enhancement of one's daily life than that of buying good pots for daily use – they are so agreeable to handle that even washing up becomes a pleasure rather than a chore!' W.A. Ismay, *Ceramic Review* 1979.

oping an idea intended to communicate with others in that intense and intimate way that the best creative work can. Collecting pots to study is particularly rewarding, as it provides the opportunity to live with a pot, to get to know it intimately, and to use it. Collecting the work of an individual or of a specific genre may lead to a visit to his studio, or the chance to become familiar with unpublished philosophies, to discover surroundings in which work was created, and perhaps to develop friendships.

Serious collectors may amass a large body of work that it is possible to study either through a private visit, or through loans to an exhibition. Some individuals donate their collections to a museum, thus preserving a body of work for others to study. It is interesting to see collectors gather at the opening of an exhibition. They will be competing to make the purchase of one or two pieces, and must decide quickly which works appeal to them most. This process of decision-making demands a good understanding of all aspects of the art of throwing if a sound decision about quality is to be made. The questions a collector may ask will help to build their knowledge and perhaps influence a decision.

With a large, specialist collection it becomes important to represent new developments in an artist's repertoire, and to try and gain an understanding of where new ideas have come from. A few collectors will base their decisions on investment potential, and in this context the largest, most prominent pieces are normally selected. Watching collectors bidding in the charged atmosphere of the auction-house sale-room is interesting, as not all prices will relate to the perceived quality of the pot, and personal value judgments are brought into question. To have the confidence to make a judgement of quality based on extensive study is to use knowledge; to base that judgement on intuition is to trust your heart: both are important.

The growth of specialist collectors of studio pottery in the twentieth century has undoubtedly had an effect on the development of pottery both in style and purpose. There was a recognition by Bernard Leach early in his career that the pots that brought the most money were those that a few collectors desired, but initially there was not sufficient demand for these to maintain a steady income. The production of a wide range of useful wares to complement the exhibition pots quickly became the format that potters adopted to meet market demand.Within the specialist exhibition market some forms would bring greater financial

Pots drying in Jim Malone's workshop. (Alex McErlain)

reward than others, for example, a large vase would sell for much more money than an equally large pitcher. A tea bowl would bring four times as much as a mug with a handle. Collectors might specialize in acquiring tea bowls and look to find examples that encapsulate the current concerns of a potter in this small-scale format. The way an exhibition is promoted via photographic images is important to the collectors, who will often try to acquire the pot which appears on the poster. In these ways the style and purpose of exhibition pots is driven by concerns that are not necessarily the prime motivation for the expression of an artist's ideas.

4 The Wheel

The potter's wheel is believed to have originated in Mesopotamia around 4000BC. The speed with which pottery could be made on the wheel undoubtedly influenced its popularity, and its use became widespread. Early wheels were probably quite slow moving, as the bearing on which the wheel spun would not have been sophisticated. The pots would have been thrown directly on the flywheel in a manner similar to that in the illustration of pottery being thrown in India in the late twentieth century.

Wheel-made pottery became the prime mode of manufacture on some continents, for example Europe and Asia, but not on others, such as South America. Nevertheless the influence of the wheel on the development of pottery form is profound, and as potters honed their throwing skills a language of expression was developed unique to the individual – so much so that if a group of potters were all to make identical vessels they would instantly be able to say who made which pot.

The historical development of the potter's wheel has seen changes of configuration and power source, but right up to the present day there has been little change in the basic elements, essentially a bearing, a flywheel, a wheel-head and a means of moving it. Visual evidence of early types of wheel exists in the form of drawings, one of the most renowned of which is an Egyptian tomb wall painting of 2400BC that shows pottery being made on simple wheels. Closer to our time, very precise drawings of two kick wheels in use were published in *Three Books of the Potter's Art* by Cipriano Piccolpasso in 1559.

Most of the developments in wheel technology are connected to the means of propelling the wheel, though some wheels in use today are hardly changed from those of thousands of years ago, simply because the wheel is essentially a simple piece of equipment. The invention of steam power and electricity brought about the biggest change from human methods of propulsion. During the twentieth century, electricity significantly affected the character of the potter's wheel by providing power without the need for a heavy flywheel, thus doing away with much of the associated physical bulk.

*P*ottery-making in India on a stone wheel. The tilted wheel is common in some countries. (Archana Choksi)

However, although power wheels are widely available, power is not always accessible, therefore in many countries wheel technology remains unchanged from earlier centuries.

It is interesting to see how some low technology societies adapt aspects of modern technology by recycling – for example they might adapt a lorry wheel into a potter's wheel by filling the tyre with sand to provide a heavy flywheel that will revolve on the lorry axle. On the other hand, some contemporary studio potters shun power-driven wheels in favour of simple hand- or foot-powered varieties, citing the intimacy of involvement with the process as the rationale for their choice.

The Wheel in Industry

The commercial manufacture of pottery wheels probably began when industry started to mass produce thrown pottery. The wheel was used

'The wheel imposes its economy, dictates limits, provides momentum and continuity. Concentrating on continuous variations of simple themes, I become part of the process; I am learning to operate a sensitive instrument which may be resonant to my experience of existence now – in this fantastic century.' Hans Coper.

extensively in eighteenth- and nineteenth-century industrial potteries before slip casting became the principal means of production. The panel illustrated, from the Wedgwood Memorial Institute, features mass-produced pottery being thrown on a wheel. This type of pottery wheel was used by the industry in Staffordshire, England. The wheel is revolved by the woman on the right-hand side turning a large driving wheel that connects via a rope to the potter's wheel featured on the left.

A potter turning a momentum wheel with a stick inserted in a hole in the wheel-head. China, 1998. (Debbie Entwistle)

Large industrial wheels, driven by an engine or electricity, are characteristically heavy duty affairs, built to withstand the rigours of extensive use and to last for many years. This sort of wheel continued to be used into the twentieth century, notably in potteries that produced garden wares, the type of work for which throwing is still the most suitable means of production. Then the development of the studio pottery movement later in the twentieth century encouraged manufacturers to produce a wider range of pottery wheels suitable for the small enterprise and for the growing number of educational establishments where throwing was being taught.

'Throwing pots': terracotta panel on the Wedgwood Memorial Institute, Staffordshire 1863–73. This building features six terracotta panels depicting the process of pottery making, designed by Matthew Eldon.

Types of Wheel

Pottery wheels are usually described according to their method of propulsion: for example, a power wheel is driven by an external source of power such as electricity; a kick wheel maintains continuity of power by the potter's foot kicking a bar; and a momentum wheel makes use of the falling speed of a heavy revolving flywheel.

The Electric Wheel

Electric wheels are the most common type of power wheel available, and come in many differing designs. The driving mechanism may involve a speed-reducing belt-and-pulley system, friction wheels or a variable speed motor. The motor and control system for electric wheels is usually housed inside a wooden or steel casing. This casing will determine to some extent the ease of portability for the wheel. Large, wooden-cased wheels are normally used in a fixed position, although they may be moved around. The designer will have fitted an adjustable seat and a large plastic tray, and hopefully will have given a general feeling of stability to the machine.

There are numerous small, steel-cased wheels on the market that are designed for ease of movement and transportability. This type of wheel will normally not have a seat and will be very low in height, enabling the potter to position a chair or stool in close proximity, or to stand whilst making a large pot. The power mechanism for an electric wheel is usually controlled by means of a pedal attached to the side of the wheel, or fitted to a movable wire to give greater flexibility.

*R*ay Finch throwing on an electric wheel; note the wheel-head is fitted with a square, removable batt.

The Kick Wheel

A kick wheel works by connecting a foot-bar to a treadle system, enabling continuous movement of the wheel-head to be maintained through kicking. Kick wheels are frequently home-made to a design tailored to individual requirements, although some commercial ones have been developed. The key factors involved in the design are the weight of the flywheel, the body position and the drive mechanism. The flywheel helps maintain movement of the wheel-head through momentum, and logically, the heavier the flywheel, the longer that movement will be maintained – although this is not always an advantage.

What is helpful is the wheel's ability to respond sensitively to any change of speed when throwing, and in respect of this it is worth observing that a very heavy flywheel will take a lot of energy to set in motion, and will be difficult to slow down or stop. In contrast, a very light flywheel will make little contribution to keeping the wheel turning, and more energy will be used in kicking. A compromise is usually sought that tries to balance sensitivity of response with energy input.

When continuous kicking is required, the potter will be most comfortable if seated, and the proximity of the seat to the wheel-head is crucial because it will affect how well he can maintain control of driving the wheel whilst throwing pots. Thus a seat positioned very close to the wheel-head will give good support for throwing, but will restrict leg movement. Once again, compromise is sought, and in this instance the height and leg length of the individual must be taken into account. Some kick wheels operate from a standing position, which is undoubtedly good for posture, avoiding a continuously bent back, but seriously compromises body support, as the potter must balance on one leg.

Drive mechanisms for propelling a kick wheel are of either direct or geared action. A direct action mechanism will turn the wheel in direct response to the speed of kicking – thus one movement of the bar will produce one revolution of the wheel-head. This type of action works quite well for most pots, though when making very small items the wheel is required to spin quickly and a furious kicking action is required.

Large pots are more difficult to make on a direct-action kick wheel as the force exerted by kicking is fighting against the pressure being exerted on a large lump of clay. One answer to this problem is to have some kind of gearing attached to the drive that can multiply the revolutions of the wheel-head in relation to the kick-bar movement. However, if the wheel-head makes two or more revolutions for one kick of the bar, it becomes difficult to operate the wheel at very slow speed. Thus the most useful geared kick wheels are those whose gearing may be easily changed.

'My wheel is really a Korean/continental hybrid: it demands sensitivity in use, and for larger pots, patience. It means you have to coax the clay to do what is required, you cannot force it. These pots have a certain character which is just not obtainable on any other sort of wheel.' Jim Malone.

The Momentum Wheel

The earliest kinds of wheel were most closely related to the modern momentum wheel. The wheel in its simplest form requires a heavy flywheel to provide the power, and a good bearing to keep it revolving as long as possible. It is this movement that is maintained by the flywheel, which allows the potter to throw for short periods whilst the wheel is continually slowing down. This 'falling momentum' requires an adjustment to the manner in which pots are thrown. Thus, heavy pressure will slow the wheel down more quickly, and using softer clay may help reduce resistance and make the pot respond to less pressure. Even so, there will probably be some breaks whilst the wheel is set in motion time and again throughout the throwing cycle, although some small bowls can be made without a second revolving action.

Momentum wheels can be driven by kicking with the foot, or by inserting a stick into a hole in the wheel-head or flywheel, enabling the potter to use arm movements to generate speed. The renowned Japanese potter Shoji Hamada used a stick-driven wheel, and film of him working inspired many studio potters to develop momentum wheels of their own. The intimate relationship between potter and wheel is very noticeable when a momentum wheel is observed in use.

The main component of the momentum wheel, the flywheel, may be made with a hollow centre, when it could be better described as a flyring. In the illustration above right, an Indian potter is seen working with a flyring made from a cartwheel. The wheel is revolved by using a stick inserted into a hole in the ring. The advantage of a flyring is that the weight is concentrated at the outside of the wheel where it will be most effective in generating momentum: it will be quicker to set in motion and easier to stop, therefore energy is not wasted.

A momentum wheel is extremely quiet in use as compared to an electric or even a kick wheel. There is no body movement once the wheel is set in motion, and concentration may be focused entirely on the work of the hands. The potter Patrick Sargent did much to popularize the use of the momentum wheel, developing a number of differing designs that took advantage of modern technology to improve performance. The Stow Sargent wheel illustrated was a joint venture he undertook with a

Indian potter throwing on a wheel-head with spokes. (Archana Choksi)

Patrick Sargent throwing on the Stow Sargent wheel. (Brian Guest)

'I use several wheels, all of the momentum pit-type turned by stick and foot. The wheel may be seen as a tool of restricted repertoire, but I like to employ it as a release, using soft clay and dying momentum to achieve a blend of irregularity with the symmetric nature inherent in the thrown form.' Patrick Sargent.

commercial manufacturer to bring precise engineering and ergonomic skills, together with a potter's personal experience, to the development of a successful batch-manufactured wheel.

Propelling the Wheel

Body movement

The action of propelling a wheel by continuous kicking puts the potter's body into a constantly moving state. This is rather disconcerting for beginners who are trying to maintain a steady hand, but with practice, a fluency of movement between hand, leg and body ensures that pots are made with ease. One side effect often attributed to throwing on a kick wheel is a constant nodding movement of the potter's head in time with the revolving wheel. Not everyone develops this 'potters nod', though Bernard Leach was seriously afflicted, and myself, too. It is always a source of amusement to students when they first watch me demonstrate. Incidentally I nod whether I am using a kick, electric or momentum wheel, so I remain unconvinced as to the origin of the nod.

Wheel Direction

An anti-clockwise movement is the most usual direction for Westerners to revolve the wheel, but in some countries, notably Japan and India, pots are thrown with the wheel turning in a clockwise direction. The hand actions during throwing are equally demanding, so the direction of wheel movement does not logically relate to a person being right- or left-handed; however, with turning it is advantageous for left-handed people to have the wheel revolving

clockwise so they can position the turning tool on the left-hand side of the pot, thus improving visibility. Some modern electric wheels can revolve in either direction at the turn of a switch. Kick and momentum wheels may be revolved either way.

Wheel Construction

Seating

The majority of pottery wheels have provision for seating, whether it be a bench into which the wheel is built, or an attached seat, or a detached one; any of these will help the potter maintain comfort and control whilst working. In some countries the potter squats at the wheel, as may be seen in the illustration of an Indian potter working. This position allows for a wheel to be constructed without a shaft to raise the level of the wheel-head, and is possibly how early wheels were used. In Egypt the tradition is for the potter to sit at the side of the wheel, rather than straddling it.

Momentum wheels are often built into a bench that the potter must sit in whilst throwing. Electric wheels usually have a seat attached to the casing, and it is helpful if this seat is adjustable in height to suit the individual. Seats will be more comfortable if they are padded, or if the potter sits on a cushion. A prolonged period spent at the wheel should be made as comfortable as possible.

Wheel Tray

Most commercially available wheels are supplied with a tray to hold a water pot, tools and catch splashes, and to contain clay trimmings. A wheel tray is also useful as an arm support during throwing. The larger the tray the better the access to the wheel-head, and the more potential there is for fitting and removing batts. Wheels without a tray are used by potters who want closer uninterrupted access to the wheel-head. Many modern electric wheels have removable trays that offer the choice of using one when required. If the wheel does not have a tray, pots must be made without too much water, as this would very quickly wet all the surroundings as well as the potter. Momentum wheels are not usually fitted with a wheel tray, but pots may be thrown from soft clay, with a minimum of water, without creating a mess.

Wheel-head

Wheel-heads are normally made from metal or wood: a metal wheel-head will be more durable, a wooden one more pleasant to touch. A wooden wheel-head is easily fashioned from hardwood or laminated water-resistant plywood, and may be more easily tailored to an individual's needs. The diameter of a wheel-head is sometimes determined by the proportions of the wheel tray. Most commercial heads are around 25cm (10in) wide, though a wider wheel-head of 45cm (17.7in) diameter is necessary if it is to be turned by a stick.

The height at which the wheel-head is set in relation to the seat is important. Many potters prefer the seat and the wheel-head to be at the same height. Some wheel-heads are adjustable in height, but a good alternative – especially if you suffer from a bad back – is to adapt raised batts to give a working height for specific forms.

Specially adapted wheel-heads to accommodate removable batts are commercially available in a variety of designs. A pegged wheel-head that locates two pegs into a drilled batt provides a simple solution; however, this requires a batt to be permanently fitted to the wheel-head.

A Wheel for Special Needs

Engineers have been inventive in making and adapting wheels to accommodate the special needs of individuals. For example, being able to position a wheelchair in close proximity to the wheel-head, and to control speed with hand levers, makes throwing possible for those individuals who cannot use leg movements. A recent design for an electric wheel (by Stow Potters Wheels, of Wales) has the drive mechanism incorporated into the wheel-head housing, so the wheel can be raised or lowered with ease; this feature, combined with a flexible adjustment for the seating position, makes the wheel adaptable to the needs of many individuals.

Points to Consider When Choosing a Wheel

- **Use**: The normal use of the wheel may affect choice: for example, a wheel used for making small porcelain bottles will not require the same degree of robustness as one for producing large quantities of big garden pots.
- **Size**: The working environment will often place some restrictions on the size of a wheel; however, most wheels do not occupy much studio space, and as the potter will spend many hours at the wheel, comfort should be given priority. Small wheels that are readily transportable are popular with those potters who regularly travel around demonstrating.
- **Torque**: This is the force that causes rotation, and is the most crucial element to consider when choosing an electric wheel. The ability of a wheel to take the pressures exerted on clay without losing speed will make the process of throwing easier: a drive system that loses torque or slips during normal working is very annoying. To test a wheel's capability, try putting pressure on the wheel-head whilst it is revolving at the slowest

Wheel-head fitted with a raised batt.

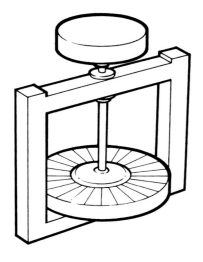

A simple momentum wheel.

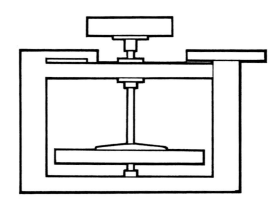
Momentum wheel, side elevation.

speed: if it stops revolving easily, the wheel is of poor quality.

- **Noise**: Some wheels are quite noisy in use, and this must be considered in relation to the time spent working on it; the quietest wheel is a momentum one. Patrick Sargent once commented: 'I remember an old film about Hamada: it showed him throwing on a stick wheel, and the only noise was the sound of clay spinning in his hands.' The rhythmic clickety-clack sound made by a kick wheel can be quite acceptable, but an electric wheel that emits a high-pitched whine will soon begin to irritate.

- **Cost**: A new electric wheel may seem expensive, but it is a modestly priced piece of equipment when considered in relation to the overall cost of pottery-making for a year. It is a better policy to invest in a quality wheel that will give good service for a few decades, than to compromise quality for cost. There are numerous suppliers of second-hand pottery equipment who sell wheels. Potters on a very tight budget may consider building a wheel, which is not a difficult task.

Building a Wheel

Some years ago a simple momentum wheel was designed and built, during the course of a week, at Manchester Metropolitan University by a group of students under the guidance of Patrick

Sargent. The wheel they designed is very simple, it has given good service, and it was cheap to build. The drawings show the principal elements, made to fit the average measurements of the student group; the dimensions can be easily modified to fit an individual. The wheel is stripped down to its bare essentials, and can be adapted to many differing situations by building it into a fixed bench or constructing a casing around it.

The rectangular frame was made from 10 × 7.5cm (4 × 3in) timber soundly jointed together. Two commercial bearings hold a steel shaft, one bearing fixed to the base, and the other underneath the top of the frame. The fly-ring, constructed from an old cartwheel and concrete, is bolted to the shaft. The distance between the wheel-head and the flywheel is critical, though the decision regarding this measurement can be delayed until everything else is constructed; then try out the wheel by sitting at it, and cut down the shaft to fit the wheel-head at the most suitable height.

The dimensions of the wheel illustrated are as follows:

Frame: 60 × 115cm (24 × 45in)
Flyring: 1m (39in) wide, 6cm (2in) thick, 25cm (10in) concrete ring
Wheel-head: 50cm (20in) wide, 10cm (4in) thick
Distance from the flywheel to the top of the wheel-head: 60cm (24in)
Distance from the seat to the top of the wheel-head: 12cm (5in)

5 Clay

'A potter's prime need is good clay. Whether he be industrial, peasant or studio potter, the raw material of which pots are made is of fundamental importance. Upon the quality of the clay depends the strength and still more the character of the finished pot.'

Bernard Leach, *A Potter's Book.*

Clay bodies influence the art of throwing in many ways, the ingredients affecting plasticity, texture, shrinkage and colour. The most plastic clays lend themselves to manipulation, but may not hold a shape easily; extremely fine clays may shrink so much that the pots become prone to cracking; coarse clays may be painful

to throw, or may split apart if stretched too much. The choice of clay, its properties and its working condition must be carefully considered. Most clays for throwing are blends of more than one clay, together with other materials, and because they are not composed of a single clay they are more accurately described as clay bodies.

Clay Bodies for Throwing

Commercial Clay Bodies

Many clay bodies are available commercially; their formulation is usually directed to a general purpose, but some are specifically developed for throwing. Clay is generally supplied in a plastic state, ready for immediate use; frequently it will have been processed through a de-airing pug mill, and may require little further treatment before throwing. Some potters buy two or three differing clays and make blends to suit their own particular purpose, and this is a good practice, because by choosing carefully, several bodies may be developed that are flexible enough to be modified, if necessary.

Most suppliers will provide small samples of clay that the purchaser may try before committing himself to larger quantities. It is also useful to consult one of the surveys that occasionally appear in specialist periodicals reviewing the clay bodies currently available and their suppliers.

A good way to test the capabilities of an unknown clay is to throw a thin bowl with a turned foot. The workable characteristics in

Jug, by Alex McErlain. Height 29cm (11.4in). Salt-glaze stoneware, 2000. The clay body for making salt-glaze ware plays a vital role in developing the glaze finish as well as affecting the character of the thrown pot.

both throwing and turning may be noted, and measurements taken to calculate shrinkage. Record the behaviour of the glazed and fired form, looking to see if the colour relates to the glazes that will be used, observing whether the form softens or distorts, and seeing if the body fuses to the batt wash on the kiln shelf; all of these observations will be significant when trying to evaluate whether a clay is suitable to your needs.

Commercial clays vary significantly in price – as a general rule the more you pay, the more involved the preparation will have been; some clay bodies are prepared by grinding, blending, filter pressing and pugging, and inevitably these clays will be more expensive than those that have not had much processing. The cheapest clays may have had little refinement and run the risk of being contaminated with lime, which can have a devastating effect on fired ware. It pays to carry out extensive trials before making a large investment in a quantity of clay.

Clay Mixing

The best way to control a clay body is to mix it yourself, if you can. There are several methods of doing this, but the availability of machinery may be the deciding factor. Specialist clay-mixing machines can quickly blend new batches and will be useful in reclaiming clay. Studio potters frequently use an old baker's dough mixer to mix clay: the process is quick, and the resultant body may be stored to improve workability. Economically, the savings made in buying powdered materials must be offset by the time taken to mix clay.

Wet Mixing

The method for mixing clay that is widely regarded as producing the best body is wet mixing. This is easily adopted for small quantities that can be mixed by hand, perhaps to test out new blends or to explore the possibilities of a natural clay. The process involves drying out the ingredients, breaking down the material so that it will be easily turned into a slip, mixing it thoroughly with water, sieving it, and finally removing the water until the body is plastic. It also ensures that the particles are blended in the finest way, and allowing it to dry out by settling produces a closely bonded body. Industry

uses a similar method to make clay but with the help of machinery: a blunger is used to make large quantities of slip, and a filter press extracts the necessary amount of water.

The problems for the studio potter with this method is the expense of purchasing and then housing the machinery. Some potters adopt the old country potter's method of mixing a large quantity of clay once a year and working with the appropriate seasons of the year to dry out the slip. Clay mixed by a wet method is usually very plastic and therefore good for throwing. Once a clay body has been mixed it should be passed through a pug mill to make the consistency more even. A de-airing pug mill will ensure the clay body is dense and free from air, which will make it possible to throw straight from the machine. Most clays benefit from wedging prior to throwing.

Grog and Fillers

A clay body may be textured by adding grog or other fillers such as sand or molochite. Grog is fired and crushed clay, and is sold in various grades ranging from fine to coarse; these grades are numbered according to the mesh size through which they may pass – thus a grog described as 30/85s will pass through a 30-mesh sieve, but not through an 85-mesh one. It is common practice to select differing particle sizes of filler so that the particles fit together densely to achieve a well compacted body. Fillers not only provide texture, but reduce shrinkage and affect body strength.

Colour

A clay body may have a natural colour deriving from one of the ingredients. Terracotta clays are the darkest of these, their colour originating from the iron content. Terracotta clay is sometimes used to modify the colour of a stoneware body, however the lower vitrification point of terracotta sometimes causes problems in stoneware bodies; it is therefore more common to see a body coloured by the addition of oxides, such as iron. In order to maintain consistency of colour over a long period, many potters choose to use synthetic iron oxide of a given strength, rather than the more variable natural iron or yellow ochre. The addition of iron will encourage reduction bodies to produce speckling, its density relating directly to the particle size of the iron.

The addition of other oxides may be useful to develop a wider range of colours, but it is important to remember that some oxides, for example manganese, will act as a flux, thus changing the body in other ways. Adding a lot of colorant may also affect working properties.

Specialist body stains provide a reliable and stable means of colouring clay, but they are very expensive. The majority of clay bodies are fairly neutral in colour, thus providing a ground for the development of colour through slip or glaze.

Storing Clay

Clay improves if it is stored in damp conditions for as long as possible before use, a process called souring; it may have a musty smell after it has been well soured. If you mix your own clay from powdered materials it should be stored for a few months prior to use. Some potters encourage the souring process by the addition of vinegar, wine or yoghurt during clay preparation. For pulling handles, well soured clay is indispensable; many potters wedge a batch of fairly stiff clay and keep it specifically for handle making.

Clay Body Recipes

Comparing clay body recipes helps in gaining an understanding of why differing bodies are composed of particular ingredients.

Fine Clay Body

Hyplas 71 ball clay	66
Grolleg china clay	33

This very simple recipe was developed to make a fine-textured body that is good to throw, pale in colour to allow for easy modification, and dense when fired to stoneware. The recipe uses a Devon ball clay for plasticity and china clay for strength, and although apparently simple, it is quite specific in the particular clays chosen, each having its own special characteristics that together form a workable body. A supplier's catalogue will list many varieties of clay, remark on their characteristics and usually provide an analysis that will help in making a choice.

Textured Clay Body

Hyplas 71 ball clay	40
Hymod AT ball clay	40
Silica sand (fine)	8
Molochite, 120s	5
Grog, 30/85s	7

By comparison, this more complex body was developed to produce a textured clay with a warm colour. Hymod AT is an iron-bearing ball clay that supplies colour to the body. Sand, molochite and grog are included to give texture, each being of a different particle size, therefore encouraging a strong bond. Sand also brings a change in the silica content of the body, which will affect both clay and glaze during the firing. Molochite – calcined china clay – contributes to the colour, texture, refractory properties, dry strength and shrinkage of the body. Grog is included primarily to reduce shrinkage.

Tableware Body

Ball clay	74
China clay	24
Cornish stone	1

This is a classic recipe developed by Harry Davis, for a really good stoneware throwing body that fires densely; Cornish stone has been introduced to help vitrification.

CB1

A variation on the tableware body recipe that includes an addition of synthetic red iron oxide, which makes the unfired clay look pink in colour and projects a tan colour in reduction. Many of the pots illustrated in the process section were made using this clay body. Clay bodies are sometimes given code numbers to help identify them; these usually have their origins in the original trial codes.

BBV ball clay	75
China clay	12.5
Nepheline syenite	12.5
Red iron oxide	1

Porcelain Body

China clay	55
Potash feldspar	25
Quartz	15
White bentonite	5

Porcelain is a clay body that becomes translucent when fired. It contains feldspar to flux the silica content, thus producing translucency. The body would not be workable without the inclusion of bentonite, which increases plasticity.

Will Levi Marshall's Throwing Body

This body is particularly suitable for oxidized stoneware.

Hyplas 71 ball clay	40
Grolleg china clay	40
Potash feldspar	15
Flint	5
White bentonite	1
Molochite 80s	5
Molochite120s	15

The Working Characteristics of Throwing Bodies

The working characteristics of a specific clay body will have implications for the thrower: for example, a very coarse body can be harsh on the potter's hands, in which case measures such as throwing with thick slurry instead of water to lubricate the clay will help. Another approach to the same problem is to use a piece of cloth to protect the hands, although this will affect the degree of sensitivity of touch; however, extremely coarse clays do lend themselves to bold treatment.

Some bodies may be very short, which means they are prone to splitting during throwing; however, such clays can be improved by ageing, or simply by modifying them with a more plastic clay. Porcelain bodies contain a lot of non-plastic ingredients, and may prove unworkable without the addition of small quantities of bentonite, an extremely plastic clay. Clays such as porcelain are sometimes

described as 'thirsty' because they require a lot of lubrication during throwing. But the problem with using an excessive amount of water during throwing is that the clay softens quickly and may not hold the thrown shape very well.

A much sought-after characteristic in a throwing body is the ability to stand up well during throwing. This means that as the clay is lifted during the early stages, it holds a shape without any tendency to sit back down on itself. A clay body that has this characteristic usually contains a quantity of fine, non-plastic material such as sand or grog of a particle size that binds closely with the plastic ingredients.

The working properties of other aspects of the making process may influence the composition of a clay body; for example, if the pots are to be once fired (also known as raw glazed) the clay must be able to withstand the glazing process without being bisque fired. Many clays can be raw glazed satisfactorily without splitting or warping; however, extremely fine bodies will be more susceptible to these problems, and may require modification to combat them.

Another issue that relates to the glazing characteristics of a clay body is the rate of absorbency at bisque stage. A body may have been modified by the addition of non-plastic material such as sand, molochite and grog in order to improve the working characteristics; but a side effect of too much filler is a reduction in absorbency at bisque stage, and the consequent implications for glaze application.

Thus there are many factors to be taken into account when developing a new clay body recipe, and to some extent a series of compromises may have to be made in order to fulfil conflicting requirements.

Clay Preparation for Throwing

Clay must be prepared for throwing to ensure it is of a suitable consistency, free from hard

> For in the Market-place, one Dusk of day,
> I watch'd the Potter thumping his wet Clay:
> And with its all obliterated Tongue
> It murmur'd – "Gently, Brother, gently, pray!"
> From the *Rubaiyat* of Omar Khayyam.

high; my own bench is 75cm (29in) high, and I am 1.82m (6ft) tall. The best way to work out the optimum height for you is to mock up a bench using concrete blocks and a paving slab and try kneading some clay. It is a good idea to live with this mock-up for a while, making minor adjustments until you are certain it is suitable for you.

The bench must be very sturdy and preferably fixed to the ground. Building blocks make good supports, and may be topped with a couple of paving slabs for a workable surface. The surface of the wedging bench needs to be absorbent. A thick layer of concrete is preferable; wood gets damp quickly and the clay begins to stick to it.

Wedging

Large blocks of clay may be efficiently wedged, although it is important to strike a balance between the quantity, and the physical effort that will be required to lift the clay repeatedly. As only half of the lump will be regularly lifted up into the air, the ease with which you can do this should be your guide as to how much to choose to wedge at one time: 9kg of clay is workable for most people. The illustration shows one method of cut wedging that is efficient in terms of minimum energy expended for maximum clay mixing.

Begin wedging by firmly throwing the clay down onto the wedging bench whilst retaining hold of it with thumbs to the upper part and fingers beneath. As the clay sticks to the bench, approximately half of the block will be left jutting upwards, enabling the piece to be cut into two equal-sized pieces which will maximise the blending process.

T all bottle, by Patrick Sargent. Height 34cm (13in). Wood-fired stoneware, 1991. 'This particular clay body has a proportion of very coarse feldspar grit added to it, which means that at about 1250°C, the little granules of feldspar start to melt and expand, forcing themselves out through the clay surface, leaving a very coarse quality.'

lumps or air pockets, and made into balls of an appropriate size for throwing. The process of preparing clay is known as wedging.

The Wedging Bench

A good wedging bench is an indispensable part of a pottery workshop: it will be used every day, and will enable a variety of tasks to be carried out with efficiency. Care must be given to choosing the right bench for the individual. The bench should be as large as possible; it will serve as a normal work surface when you are not wedging, and will never be wasted space. The height of the bench should be related to the person using it: too low, and it will induce back problems; too high, and you will not be able to use the weight of your body efficiently when pushing down on the clay. Benches are generally between 70 and 80cm (27 to 31in)

Position the cutting wire at the point where the clay meets the bench, cutting upwards at an angle of 45 degrees, moving away from you.

Allow the cut half of the block to roll forwards so that the two cut surfaces of clay are facing you. Visually examine the cut surfaces for signs of trapped air, foreign bodies and lines that may show differing coloured clays being intermixed. Notice the sharp ridge at the top of the bloc.

The block of clay must be raised and thrown firmly down onto this ridge so that air is expelled as the two pieces of clay merge into one. Lift your arms high to make use of the weight of the clay when bringing it back down.

The pieces of clay should now be joined firmly together and appear as one.

If this is not the case, then they have not been thrown down hard enough. Lift the block up from one side: it will peel away from the bench easily providing the bench is absorbent and not too wet.

Turn the block through 90 degrees so that the wire will now pass through in a different direction. Grip the block firmly with the thumbs to the top, and bring it down onto the bench ready to begin the process once more.

When to Stop Wedging

As wedging progresses the clay becomes more consolidated: there should be no visible air pockets when a wire is passed through. If mixing hard clay with softer clay, the cut surfaces will at first show a difference in consistency through visible lines or strata; these lines will disappear as the wedging progresses. A good test for evenness is to run a fingertip across a freshly cut surface: the fingertips are very sensitive, so any difference in texture will be easily detected. When preparing clay for a throwing session, make sure the wedged clay is kept wrapped in plastic to prevent it from drying on the surface; this happens easily, and will seriously affect the working characteristics. Do not make up too many balls of clay, as these may dry out and will then need re-wedging before throwing.

Kneading or Spiral Wedging

Many potters follow the wedging process, with kneading as a final preparation for throwing,

although kneading is a good alternative to wedging if the clay is in a reasonably even condition. Wedging uses less energy if you have a lot of uneven clay to prepare. To knead clay, begin by selecting a suitable quantity: for most people this will weigh between 2 and 5kg (4 and 11lb). It is important to have a manageable quantity when learning – very small and very large lumps are more difficult to knead.

Position yourself to maximize the use of the upper body when exerting force, placing the left leg in front of the right leg with the legs slightly apart so that a rocking motion may be set in place, enabling you to lean into the clay being kneaded. The process of kneading is a continuous, rhythmic action; it is difficult to describe adequately, so the following points may prove helpful:

Both hands are involved in the process, one hand guiding whilst the other controls the action. Work on about a third of the lump, allowing the other two thirds to move around, forming the distinctive spiral shape.

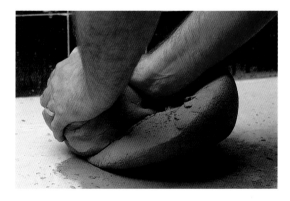

Push into the clay with the right hand using the edge of the palm and exerting thrust from the shoulder. If you exert thrust from the elbow and wrist you may tire quickly.

*R*ay Finch kneading clay.

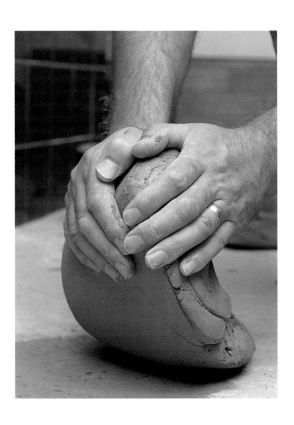

Rock the lump backwards to reposition the right hand before pushing in once more.

When finishing, keep the motion going, but stop pressing in with the right hand; this will result in the clay rolling up into a cone shape that may be thrown straight onto the wheel.

There are other related kneading techniques; one that uses both hands to push the clay is known as 'ram's head kneading'.

Foot wedging is common in the Far East, and is a viable option for studio potters to mix clay if no machinery is available. It is essentially the kneading process done on a large scale, and uses the weight of the body to provide the necessary force.

Foot wedging in China, 1998. (Debbie Entwistle)

Wedging In Grog

The addition of grog or other fillers may be done during the wedging process. It is important to weigh the clay and filler so that you may repeat the mixture with accuracy. Cut the clay into small lumps, roll each in grog until it is evenly distributed, then begin to work the lumps together by hand before commencing wedging. The grog will at first prevent the clay sticking together, but firm pressure will soon resolve this. For kneading grog in, put a layer on the bench and work over it; as kneading progresses the grog will become incorporated.

Wetting Down or Drying Out Clay

Time spent preparing clay is never wasted: the consistency of the body is easily modified, and throwing will be much easier if the clay is in an appropriate condition. Clay that is too soft is easily stiffened by cutting it into thin slices and laying it out so that air may dry it. An alternative method is to wedge on a plaster slab: this will absorb moisture, although it still runs the risk of plaster contamination. Adding grog stiffens clay, as does the addition of powdered clay, which may be possible if you mix your own body and know the proportions to add.

To soften clay that is too stiff, the easiest method is to blend in some soft reclaim clay by wedging. An alternative method is to slice the clay thinly, push the fingertips into the surface and cover with water. Leaving the water on the

Patrick Sargent's Clay Body Recipe

Westerwald ball clay	60
China clay	20
Nepheline syenite	20
Quartz	10
Salt-free vinegar	1ltr (1.75 pints)

add 1 per cent red iron oxide.

'I mix all my clay by foot; I have no machines. It has become a rhythmic ritual so essential and stimulating to the process that I really couldn't do it any other way. The vast spiral created when a clay mix is completed relates closely to the swirl from a slow wheel. By mixing it myself I can generate a clay with life and density that suits my way of throwing.' Patrick Sargent.

Weighing out clay.

clay will not make much difference, as the stiff clay acts as a non-absorbent barrier; so a certain amount of hand wedging of each small piece is the quickest way to soften small quantities. If the quantities are large, lay strips of clay between wet cloths and leave for a few days.

Try to acquire the habit of weighing out your clay, even if you are not intending repetition throwing, because this helps you to monitor your progress in acquiring skill. Cut the clay into strips to enable blocks of approximately the right size to be formed. Weigh the clay, taking care not to put air into the ball as it is formed by patting between the hands. Larger lumps are best kneaded or rolled into shape. Clay balls should be made uniform, without holes or large indents; they will be grasped with wet hands, and should not require any further working before throwing.

Most potters keep a record of the weights and dimensions of pots that they make repeatedly. The size and weight may provide a useful guide with which to estimate for a new form. The table opposite shows some specific sizes for pots that are frequently made. Obviously variation in design may have an effect on these sizes, but they do provide a useful starting point for the beginner.

Clay Reclamation

A by-product of throwing will be a quantity of soft clay scraps cut from the pot during making. There are usually a few abandoned forms from every session, too, sometimes referred to as 'dead bodies'. The turning process produces quantities of quite hard clay shavings that need recycling, and it is quite possible to reclaim clay as you go along without too much trouble, simply by wedging. A bin of fresh turnings and scraps from each day's making can be covered with a damp cloth to enable the softer scraps to damp the turnings, producing clay that may be easily wedged. Large amounts of dry clay should be put into a bin and covered with water to slake down. Gradually removing the water from the surface as the clay settles will leave a soft clay slop that can be dried in bisque-fired bowls. Cover the bowls with a cloth so the slop can stiffen without drying out on the surface. When the clay is hard enough it may be pugged or wedged ready for use once more.

S*ixteen bowls, by Debbie Entwistle. Diameter 11.5cm (4.5in). Earthenware, 2000.*

Thrown sizes and weights for making some common pottery forms

Form	width	(cm/in)	height	(cm/in)	weight	(grams/oz)
Small bowl	15	(16in)	7.5	(13in)	420	(14.8oz)
Cereal bowl	17	(6.6in)	7.5	(3in)	600	(21oz)
Pasta bowl	22.5	(8.8in)	9	(3.5in)	1,100	(38.8oz)
Breakfast cup	11.5	(4.5in)	9	(3.5in)	350	(12oz)
Saucer	18	(7in)			450	(15.8oz)
Coffee mug	11	(4.3in)	10	(3.9in)	400	(14oz)
Half pint (300ml) jug	9	(3.5in)	11	(4.3in)	350	(12oz)
One pint (550ml) jug	10	(3.9in)	15	(5.9in)	500	(17.6oz)
Side plate	20	(7.8in)			600	(21oz)
Dinner plate	29	(11.4in)			1,700	(60oz)
Large fruit plate	43	(17in)			6,500	(229oz)
Small baking dish	21	(7.6in)	9	(3.5in)	1,600	(56oz)
Large baking dish	33	(13in)	6.5	(2.5in)	3,000	(106oz)

6 Tools

Throwing tools are essentially very simple, in that their purpose is merely to extend the possibilities for developing shape and finish that cannot be achieved with the hands alone. In this respect it is interesting that tools discovered in a potter's workshop during archeological excavations and dated to the late bronze age, bore a remarkable similarity to those that potters use today.

The most useful tools are those that are perfectly suited to a given task. Most potters choose to make at least some tools themselves, customizing the design and in the process bringing a personal aesthetic to the form. Commercially manufactured tools try to accommodate a number of general approaches to making, adopted by individual potters. When visiting a studio, observation of the tools kept by an individual potter gives an insight into their approach, and frequently prompts ideas that can be adapted to your own work.

It is worth investing in good quality tools: they could well last most of your working life, and therefore work out to be relatively cheap.

Care of the Potter's Hands

The hands may be considered the most important tools used for making pots, and so it makes good sense to care for them, and to treat quickly any condition that may develop. Skin and nail problems are frequently experienced by throwers: for instance, dry or chapped and broken skin is usually caused by not drying the hands properly after throwing has finished. A good application of an appropriate hand cream at the end of each day helps to maintain skin in good condition. Worn nails occur from applying pressure to the wheel-head rather than the clay during centring; this is a common occurrence with beginners, and care must be taken to avoid this – it is better to use a wooden rib to cut the clay at the point where it meets the wheel-head, to avoid undue nail wear.

A Basic Range of Tools

A tool kit will evolve during the development of a repertoire of making, since the potter will keep adding to it as he needs different tools that are appropriate to the task in hand. Nevertheless, a basic range of tools is usually replicated in most kits, and will almost certainly include examples similar to the ones illustrated here.

A Brushes: Used mostly for applying slip, on either wet or leather-hard clay. The fat, round brushes known as mops hold a lot of thick slip and are useful for covering large areas. The key issues with a brush are its relative softness and the volume of hair. Soft hair leaves no evidence of brush marks or scratchy lines on the surface of the slip; however, some brushes are designed to leave behind strong traces of their bristles as decorative marks, with slip applied in a coarse manner known as hakeme. The volume of brush hair relates to the quantity of slip or pigment that a brush will hold. A brush with a generous amount of bristle will mean that a pot can be covered quickly because the brush will not require frequent reloading.

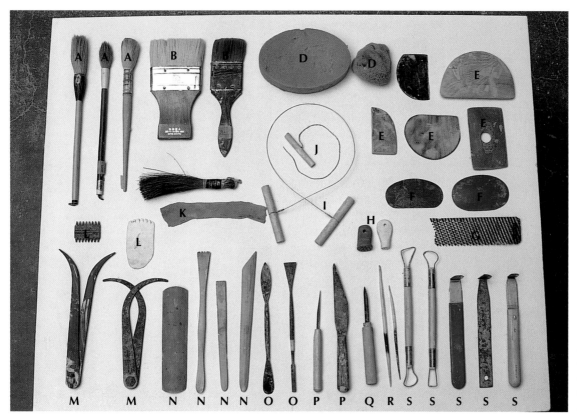

A selection of the author's pottery tools, some he made himself, others purchased from suppliers.

A plate being slipped with a wide, soft-haired brush.

and compress the surface of the clay or to help define form, rather than as a profile. The term 'rib' probably derives from the practice of using a cow's rib bones for making tools in country potteries of the eighteenth and nineteenth centuries. Many contemporary potters use old credit cards fashioned into throwing ribs.

F   Kidneys made from steel and rubber: Finishing tools used to create very smooth, or even burnished surfaces. When purchasing from a commercial supplier, choose a kidney with a great deal of flexibility as the tool is normally used on leather-hard clay and needs to give as well as resist.

G   A surform blade: A woodworking tool useful for removing large quantities of clay without exerting much pressure. It is very useful when turning porcelain to remove the initial bulk of the clay quickly yet with delicacy. The tool is good for making flat surfaces, as in faceting; it leaves behind a distinctive pattern that can be removed easily with a steel kidney, if desired.

B   Large flat brushes: Good for covering the insides of bowls or plates.

The interior of the illustrated bowl by Jim Malone was thickly coated with white slip, and a very coarse-haired brush dragged through it, displacing some of the slip and leaving behind brush marks. The potter uses this surface as a background on which to paint, using manganese and cobalt oxide, and this approach produced an image reminiscent of looking into a stream with water flowing over weeds. The unglazed rim of the pot frames the drawing and betrays evidence of wood firing where ash has been deposited on the rim.

C   The coarse brush: Made from the bristles of a floor-sweeping brush, bound together with cord; it is used for hakeme brush work, where the bristles do leave a mark.

D   Sponges: Almost indispensable to the potter. A large, synthetic sponge is required for the many instances when water and slurry must be quickly removed to leave a clean working environment. The small natural sponge is used for removing water from the inside of pots; it holds a lot of liquid, and does not leave marks in the way synthetic sponges do. A sponge may be attached to a stick to facilitate the removal of water from narrow-necked pots.

E   Ribs: May be made from hardwood or plastic, slate, bone or even fired clay. The shapes are usually developed for specific curves. Ribs are normally used as a finishing tool to smooth

Jim Malone's range of brushes and other tools on the workbench. (Alex McErlain)

*S*hallow bowl, by Jim Malone. Width 33cm (13in). Reduced stoneware, 1994.

*U*nomi, by Bill Marshall. Height 10cm (4in). Reduced stoneware, 1980. This small drinking cup, called a unomi, has been decorated with white slip using a coarse-haired brush to deposit a thick layer with brush marks strongly in evidence. The brush marks impart a powerful decorative image showing spirited movement.

H   Stamps or seals: Made from bisque-fired clay. A personal seal with carved initials (in reverse) or a monogram is better made in red clay and bisque-fired so that it will be both durable and absorbent. Plaster seals break easily, bringing the risk of plaster contamination to the clay.

I   A cutting wire: May be made from steel or brass wire, or sometimes nylon line. The toggles attached to the ends make the tool easy to use during throwing, when the hands may be covered in slurry. For convenience in use the length of the wire should equal the diameter of the wheel-head plus the width of two hands; this will enable any form to be cut off. A twisted wire will ease the removal of a wet pot, the twist helping to prevent the cut clay from resealing itself; it will also leave a decorative mark on the base of the pot.

J   A cutting cord: May be made from twisted thread, with a toggle fixed at one end. The cord is used for cutting off pots made by throwing from a hump of clay. The cord is laid into a groove, allowed to wrap itself around the pot, and then pulled out rapidly, resulting in a clean and level cut.

K   Chamois leather: Used for compressing and smoothing the rim of a pot. When wrapped over the edge of a freshly thrown pot, its fine texture produces a smooth, dense surface that is difficult to obtain in any other way and is particularly appropriate to the rim of a cup.

L   Combs: Made from wood, plastic, rubber or metal; used for decorating, often through a

slip. The teeth may be cut to differing sizes, and the end of the tool curved to prevent the comb from digging in to the clay.

M   Callipers: Made from plastic or metal; required for measuring lid fittings. They must be easy to adjust, and stay locked in place. The smaller sizes available are the most useful, as the majority of measurements taken will be relatively small.

N   Wooden modelling tools: Easily made from hardwood or bamboo. They are normally used for fine modelling, scoring or decorating.

O   Steel modelling tools: Useful for decorating; they cut through clay very easily, leaving a sharp line.

P   A potter's knife: Should have a blade of a single thickness, and not tapered (like the blade of a cutlery knife). A single-thickness blade cuts cleanly, without spreading the clay apart. Most potters have two knives, one with a small, firm blade for general work, and one with a long, flexible blade useful for cutting a teapot spout or for faceting.

Q   Hole cutter: For piercing a grid of holes in a teapot. Tapered versions allow holes of differing size to be made.

R   Porcupine quills: Used for very fine tasks, such as trimming the top of an uneven pot, or bursting the occasional air bubble; they are an alternative to a steel spike or needle, both of which are dangerous if they get lost in the clay. Ask your local zoo for quills that the porcupine has shed.

S   Turning tools: Made from bent steel and hooped wire; they provide an efficient cutting edge for turning leather-hard clay. It is a good idea to keep a variety of turning tools of differing sizes and shapes to choose from.

The Kiln as Tool

The ultimate potter's tool is a kiln: it may be viewed as an equal contributor in the creative process of making, and not just as a means of developing glaze and rendering work permanent. The modern movement in wood firing treats the kiln as a tool, to be used to develop a

Sgraffito drawing through wet slip.

Stoneware cider jar, by Ray Finch. Height 49cm (19in). Reduced stoneware, 1988. The pot has been dipped into an iron-bearing slip, and combed to produce the linear pattern. The slip has changed the colour of the glaze, the combed lines revealing the clay body beneath the slip.

Salt-glaze, stoneware ink bottle made by the Doulton company. Height 22cm (8.6in). Nineteenth century. The neck and shoulder of the pot have been faceted when the clay was leather hard. The cutting has produced a distinctive square neck that has twisted during the firing. Ink bottles were made in vast quantities, and the salting process was a very economical means of glazing them.

range of expressive characteristics, taking advantage of the manner in which the kiln operates, namely by melting materials onto the pots at extreme temperatures. A thorough understanding of the way the kiln responds to stoking; the arrangement of pots within the chamber to direct the passage of flame; the behaviour of melting clay and glaze: all of these factors contribute to the vision of a kiln as a tool to be used in the creative expression of ideas.

7 Process, Beginning to Make Pots

The art of throwing demands a high degree of skill, usually acquired over a long period of time. It is possible to teach someone the rudiments of throwing in a day, indeed I do this on a regular basis in the university where I teach, and have not yet found anyone who cannot be taught the basics to enable them to produce a pot of sorts. Developing beyond this takes commitment, patience and encouragement, but those who keep trying will be rewarded with a whole new language with which to express themselves.

When learning to throw it is better to try and make something specific, rather than just accept what comes along. In this way a structure may be applied to the method, and results can be compared for signs of improvement. Making a simple bowl for pasta is a good way for beginners to learn to make pots; the language of the form is adaptable to a whole range of useful bowls, and offers endless variations for developing style. By having a specific form to aim towards, the beginner will become more involved with the process of throwing, and will have some criteria by which to measure achievement.

A bowl form expands in the direction of the centrifugal forces created by the spinning wheel, consequently this is the easiest form to manipulate in wet clay. As with most objects, the easiest to practically make is also the most demanding visually, and making a good bowl is one of the most difficult tasks the potter must master. Physically a pasta bowl, designed to hold an individual portion, needs to be of an appropriate scale to contain the food, and wide enough to allow it to be manipulated. The meal is not notably delicate, and the volume of food is considerable. Visually the form should be generous to allow the pot to be seen as well as the pasta. The foot must be broad, to give support in use, and some thought should be given to the way the bowls may stack, as normally several will need to be stored.

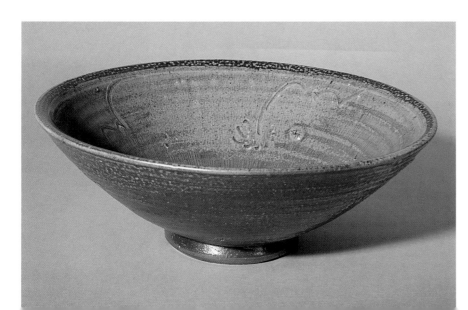

Pasta bowl, by Alex McErlain. Width 20cm (8in). Salt-glaze stoneware, 2000.

Throwing

Making a Pasta Bowl

Material: Fine clay body: Hyplas 71 ball clay 66 per cent, Grolleg china clay 33 per cent.

Weight and thrown size: 1.1kg (2.4lb) of clay; width 22.5cm (8.8in) × height 9cm (3.5in).

Making:
The process of making begins with throwing the clay firmly onto the wheel-head. The latter must be damp – not wet or dry, but damp – for the clay to adhere. Use a sponge to dampen it, wiping away excess moisture, then throw the ball of clay firmly into the centre; if it lands a long way off centre, either remove it and try again, or push it closer to the centre.

The easiest way to open out the ball is by pushing in the thumb. The grip may seem ungainly at first; notice how the fingers of the right hand are pointing towards the body, with the thumb appearing to rest across the top of the clay ball. The left hand supports the outside of the ball.

The first stage of throwing is called centring: the clay must be lubricated with a layer of water, so the water pot should be placed close to the wheel-head on the right-hand side (for a right-handed person). The ideal shape in which to centre clay may be described as a mushroom shape, in which the base is narrow and the top domed. One hand should push downwards whilst the other presses inwards. Always get hold, and let go of the clay gently, putting pressure on in between. Snatching hold of the clay will push the ball further off centre, and letting go too quickly will have the same result.

    The natural inclination of the spinning wet lump of clay is to move with centrifugal force towards the perimeter of the wheelhead. Centring must work to gently coax the clay into a format that stops the force from pulling the clay off centre. It is important to try and support the arms during these early stages either by leaning on the wheel tray or by pressing the arms into the sides of the body to give support.

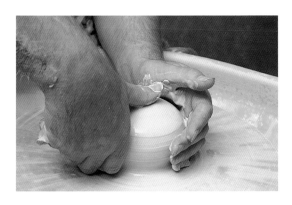

As the thumb is pushed downwards, a curved interior shape is formed, already appearing to be the right shape for a bowl. The clay rides up between the thumb and fingers, which gives great control of the emerging form. The left hand is still pressing on the outside, helping to keep the clay centred.

Keeping the same grip and with one continuous movement, the right hand squeezes the clay, making the

first lift, bringing about a thick-walled bowl shape. This operation is very bold, and can be brutal if carried out too quickly, tearing off the entire pot from the wheel-head; it is therefore important to take your time.

Note the position of the water pot by the wheel-head.

The right hand should now be positioned outside the pot, with the left hand inside. The fingertips are grouped together, and will move gently up the wall of the pot whilst squeezing the clay. Note how the thumb of the left hand is in contact with the right hand, giving an added sense of stability. The ridge of clay being lifted may be seen clearly on the inside of the bowl.

It is very important to control the rim at this stage: the fingertips should gently grip the rim inside, outside and on the top, to compress it.

Rims may develop a wobble in the early stages brought about not by wobbly movement of the hands but by inaccuracy in the earlier stages of opening out. Any inaccuracy will automatically manifest its self eventually in a wobbly rim. If the problem is really bad it is better to start again. Small wobbles may be corrected through compression, more serious wobbles require cutting away some of the rim with a spiked tool. This may be carried out with a porcupine quill, cutting from the outside of the pot whilst supporting the wall on the inside with the fingers of the left hand.

By removing water with a natural sponge it will be much easier to see the form of the bowl at this stage. A continuous curve is the aim, so that the form appears strong, and so it is easy to get food out of the bowl when eating.

A curved wooden rib is used to define the inner surface of the bowl. The rib may be manipulated down the inside from rim to base, or up from the base to the rim. The rib should be used as a finishing tool, and not as a profile former. The index finger of the left hand provides additional support, to steady the operation.

A square-ended bamboo stick is used to remove clay from the base, and to facilitate lifting the pot from the wheel. Begin undercutting the base by pressing the tool onto the wheel-head, and then pushing into the pot; in this way clay will be removed onto the tool, and not forced back onto the pot. Always carry out this operation prior to finalizing the form, as it may disturb the shape.

Finishing the rim with a piece of wet chamois leather wrapped around the edge will smooth and compress the clay and help define the form; the rim on this bowl curves slightly outwards.

When cutting off the pot from the wheel-head note how the cutting wire should be gripped with the toggles to the outside of the fists, the wire tensioned on the wheel-head by pressing down with the thumbs. The wheel-head should be kept revolving to avoid distorting the pot with the drag of the wire: ideally it should make one revolution whilst the wire passes through the clay, and the operation should be carried out swiftly and confidently, passing the wire away from the body. Note how the wheel-head is quite clean near to the base of the pot.

To lift the pot off, first place the fingertips of both hands at the far side of the bowl, and push gently upwards: the pot will begin to rise up, allowing the middle fingertips to be placed underneath; finally bring both little fingers onto the base of the pot and lift it cleanly up, away from the body. Do not worry about the rim distorting a little during this operation – it will fall back into place on its own if it isn't touched.

The bowl should be placed down onto a clean board in reverse order of lifting: first the front edge should touch the board, then the middle fingers are withdrawn, and finally the index fingers. The bowl should remain round as long as you have not been too heavy-handed. If the bowl has distorted badly, do not touch it on the wall or rim, but exert pressure at the base opposite the distorted area; this will in effect distort the form in the opposing direction, thus allowing you to coax it back to round.

The wheel-head will have the remains of some clay where the pot was lifted away; this is ideal for sticking down the next ball of clay, and should be left where it is.

Ware Boards

Many differing materials may be used for making ware boards; however, the boards must be flat and must remain flat, so this rules out materials that will warp as a consequence of getting wet. The best boards are slightly absorbent so that the pot bases dry at the same rate as the walls. The scale of ware boards must relate to the working situation, and should take into account the racking needed for storage as well as the area in close proximity to the wheel. Boards will get wet, and will need to be scraped and wiped down regularly, so a durable material is desirable. Plywood designed for exterior use is durable under these conditions and may be cut to size easily. Some potters use composite roofing slates available from builder's merchants, as these are cheap and effective as ware boards.

The most important thing to say about ware boards is 'keep them clean': the pot has had all sorts of care and attention given to the surface finish, and this finish is easily destroyed by placing the pot on a dirty ware board. It is good practice to clean all ware boards before commencing a making cycle.

Make sure that your hands are clean and dry; then exert pressure at the base of the pot, keeping the wrists fairly close together and the fingers wrapped as far round the base as possible. Keep the thumbs out of the way, and lift boldly. The pot should remove easily from the wheel-head and not distort very much.

Lifting Pots from the Wheel

Bowl shapes may be lifted easily as described, unless they are too wide, in which case a batt must be used to throw the pot on. There are variations to the practice of lifting: for example, some potters slide the work off the wheel-head on a film of water. The simpler and more direct the practice, the less time need be devoted to the task. More vertical forms require a different method of lifting: the surface of such a form should be cleaned of slurry by running a stick or rib down it – if the pot is wet, the hands will slip when trying to grip it.

At first a few pots may get squashed as the fear of destroying work overrides concentration on the task. The pot should be placed on a clean board, close to a previously made pot, thus utilizing shelf space efficiently. In the photograph it may be clearly seen how the little fingers grip the pot at the base, with the other fingers having minimal contact. The adjacent pot shows the marks made by lifting: these are easily removed when the pot is leather hard.

Batts

There are some pots that cannot be successfully lifted from the wheel when freshly thrown, and they must be made on a removable batt. As the width of a pot increases in relation to its height, so does the difficulty of lifting it off. Batts can be made from a range of materials, for example wood, slate, tile or even clay. They are fitted to the wheel-head either by fixing with clay, or may be held in a batt holder designed specifically so that a batt will slot into it easily. Some wheels are fitted with a special wheel-head to hold a batt.

When making very wide pots, a batt that is wider than the wheel-head has to be fitted; it may even need to be raised to extend above the wheel tray. Batts of differing heights are known as raised batts, and help the potter maintain a good posture during throwing because he can keep his back straight. Other reasons for making on a batt may include being able to invert the work before it is cut off. Wide bowls and plates may be turned over more easily if a batt is placed on the rim before inverting.

In the illustration of Ray Finch throwing, bowls are being made on square batts set into a specially made wooden holder. This is a cheap and quick way to make batts, though care must be taken with this design, not to be hit by the

*R**ay Finch throwing shallow bowls.*

revolving sharp corners. The stick fixed to the wheel tray will indicate the height and width of the bowl. Ray is a master of the art of throwing; he always makes pots in batches in order to get into a rhythm and understand the form he is trying to achieve, even though he may have made the shape thousands of times before: it is always treated as a new, unique pot.

Turning

The process of turning (also known as trimming) has as much creative potential as the art of throwing. With some pots, turning involves little development of the thrown form, and is simply a tidying-up operation. On some thrown pots the form is unintelligible before turning. The nature of the clay body, be it fine or coarse, the condition of the clay – soft or leather hard – and the choice of cutting tools, all contribute to this creative process.

'Lathe turning pots': terracotta panel on the Wedgwood Memorial Institute, Burslem, Staffordshire; 1863–73. This building has six long panels depicting the process of pottery making in industry, designed by Matthew Eldon. This panel features pottery being finished by turning on a lathe; the pots were usually turned all over, and frequently included decorative linear banding.

Vase, stamped 'Powell Whitefriars Wedgwood'. Height 21cm (8in). Black basalt, c1900. An industrially produced vase, turned on a lathe and burnished. The precision characteristics of lathe-turned pottery are particularly appropriate to the production of basalt ware.

Spanish dish. Width 21cm (8in). Tin-glazed earthenware; nineteenth century. The foot on this dish has been lightly turned, and the centre pressed in revealing the cord cutting mark.

In this group of leather-hard bowls resting upside down on a clean board, the difference between the unturned bowls and the one with the turned foot is considerable. Most of the bowl form is complete, except for a thick band of clay at the base from which the foot will be turned.

Turning begins with centring the pot on the wheel-head. The easiest way to place a pot quickly in centre is to tap it with one hand whilst the wheel is revolving. Professional potters all use this skill, which takes a little practice to acquire. The bowl illustrated is a good shape to learn the centring skill, being shallow and wide at the point of contact with the wheel-head. To begin with, place the pot as close as possible to the centre of a clean and dry wheel-head – if necessary, use lines drawn on the wheel-head to help. The wheel must revolve at a constant moderate speed. Here, the right hand is being used to tap, but either hand may be used; the left hand is positioned to catch the pot should it be hit too hard and begin to fly from the wheel. The base edge of the hand and little finger are used to strike the pot, which should be hit regularly and rhythmically as it revolves. By hitting rhythmically the pot will begin to move a little with each tap. The blows must be progressively lightened to move the pot less and less each time, until eventually it sits in the centre of the wheel. It helps to concentrate on the rhythmic movements, rather than trying to catch the pot where it protrudes.

This process, like kneading, is harder to describe in words than to demonstrate in practice.

The pot is attached to the wheel with small pieces of clay or a coil of clay. There are other methods of fixing the pot, such as using suction from a damp wheel-head, or supporting the pot on a pad of clay, but for the beginner, the simplest method is to use some clay bits. Make sure the pot does not move whilst sticking the clay down, by supporting it with one hand.

A hooped turning tool is effective for the first stage of removing clay. The tool should be gripped firmly, close to the cutting edge; the fingertips of the left hand press down to give support to the pot. Note how the thumbs make contact with each other to give added support.

Clay may be removed in either a downward or upward direction, the initial aim being to remove the excess. As turning progresses, the form begins to develop in relation to the thrown shape.

In order to hollow the base a different grip is adopted, the tool now held between thumb and fingers, rather like a pen when writing. This brings the cutting edge of the tool into the correct position for removing clay. Begin in the centre of the foot and work outwards, being careful to stop in time – it is a good idea to mark the place to stop by cutting a groove at the outer edge before you begin hollowing. The shavings should come away from the pot in long, clean strips: if the clay is too hard, the shavings *will be broken or bitty, and the task made much more difficult. If the clay is too soft to turn, it will not cut cleanly and will simply clog up the tool. Notice how the grog in this clay body produces scratchy lines when being turned.*

The foot is completed with fine detailing, the shavings diminish in size, and a finger is rested on the foot-ring to help steady the tool.

A bent steel turning tool is used to complete the definition of the pot – a tool of this type will produce a smoother finish than a hooped wire. The tool is gripped firmly in the palm of the hand and held close to the cutting edge. Even at this late stage a fingertip trails on the foot-ring, and the thumbs make contact to aid sensitivity between pot and process.

Always remove the pot from the wheel to inspect the relationship between the foot-ring and the pot. The pot

will look completely different when stood the right way up. With practice it is easy to detach and re-attach the pot, so get used to looking at your work in this way.

Methods of Fixing Pots to the Wheel-head

Turning on a Pad

In production throwing, a common method of fixing pots to the wheel-head is to lay down a soft pad of clay to press the pot in to hold it. The method has several advantages: when dealing with a group of pots of similar size, they will all fit into the depression and do not require further centring; the entire outside of the form is visible, which helps considerably when viewing the turned foot in relation to the rest of the pot; and the rim is protected from damage by the soft pad of clay.

Another development for turning on a pad of clay is to remove a section to accommodate a raised part of the rim, for example a lip.

Fixing with Suction

This method relies on a good connection between the rim of the pot and the wheel-head. To stick a pot down, the wheel-head is made damp and the pot centred, before pressing firmly to the wheel, causing the damp clay to adhere with suction. Pots fixed in this way will stay attached to the wheel-head during turning, the technique having the advantage of speed and versatility. One disadvantage is the possibility of damaging delicate rims. Some degree of confidence is required to get used to the pot spinning without anything apparently holding it in place.

*C*hinese Sung dynasty bowls with delicately turned feet.

*S*hallow dish. Width 40cm (15.7in). Chinese porcelain decorated with red enamel. The wide foot-ring on a dish like this must be cut deeply to enable the glaze to clear the kiln shelf without sticking. Placing a straight-edge across the foot-ring will show the clearance. Some wide, footed dishes have a small button of clay left in the middle to support the centre during firing.

Turning on a Batt

For very wide pots such as big plates it is necessary to fix a batt to the wheel-head. Lifting the plate upside down onto the wheel may easily damage the rim, therefore it is good practice to put the batt on top of the plate (which has also been made on a batt) and grip both the batts with the plate sandwiched in between to invert it. The plate and batt must now be centred together on the wheel-head. Tiny pellets of clay placed on the wheel-head will enable the batt to be gripped when it is centred. If the wheel-head is studded, centring is made easy. There is usually enough weight in a plate to stop it moving during turning without further fixing.

Turning with a Chuck

Pots that will not support themselves upside down must be turned in a specially made pot called a chuck. A chuck should be wide in the base for stability, and thrown thick in section so it can be used many times without breaking. The profile is usually concave to provide support for the pot, that fits inside. With a narrow-necked pot the chuck supports its shoulder and provides stability during turning. A chuck is at its best when leather hard, as the clay body will be sensitive to gripping the pot; however, it will still work well when dry, and may even be bisque-fired.

A range of sizes will prove useful for general purposes, although certain pots will require a custom-made chuck.

Pots with an uneven rim may be turned on a hump of clay that is also sometimes called a

*T*wo chucks.

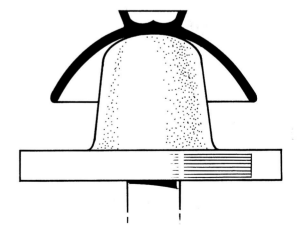

A pot being supported on a hump for turning.

chuck. The interior of the pot sits on the hump with the rim not touching anything, and in this way even very delicate porcelain bowls may be effectively turned without damaging the fine rim.

Thrown and Cut Feet

Some pots may have a foot thrown on at a later stage, bringing about the possibility of creating shapes that are not possible to cut. A coil of clay is attached to the underside of the pot and thrown into shape; it may be cut to give the appearance of a turned foot if so desired. With a very large plate it may be advantageous to throw the pot thinner in the base, and to add on a foot later, to avoid the problems associated with compression cracking with a very thick base. A thrown foot can be made taller than is possible with cutting, and may be developed into a stem form. Cutting notches in a foot-ring brings about more creative possibilities (*see* Teapot Making).

*E*wer. Height 19cm (7.5in). 600–400BC. Earthenware, unglazed. Cyprus. Made from a fine buff clay painted with iron, this pot must have been supported in a chuck to turn the delicate foot-ring.

*B*owl with decoratively cut foot-ring, by Will Levi Marshall. Width 15cm (6in). Oxidized stoneware, 1996. The cutting on this foot is intended to contribute to the dynamic nature of the distorted form.

8 Developing Technique

The bowl form provides a good basis for learning the art of throwing, but once the rudiments have been acquired it is interesting to develop a few new techniques so that a variety of forms may be made, building on the skills already developed. This chapter will deal with methods of making groups of similar pots, and transforming them through the addition of a handle or lip. The bowl forms the basis of many pots, including cup, mixing bowl, colander, pedestal bowl and sauce boat, and these all help to extend the range of skills that a thrower must acquire. The development of a bowl into a more defined article also raises awareness of a new set of design issues.

Tea bowl, by Jim Malone. Width 13cm (5in). Reduced stoneware, 1995. Made by throwing off the hump.

Throwing from a Hump

A method of making that is common in the Far East, is to throw a number of pots from one large hump of clay. It is useful for beginners to learn this method as it is a really good technique for making bowls of a similar scale but with variety in design. The method is also commonly used for making lids and very small items, because it is so much easier than centring a tiny ball of clay. It is possible to make identical pots with this method, though not as easy as when using individually weighed balls. The

large mound of clay should be patted roughly into centre – it is only necessary to centre accurately the clay at the top of the hump, that will be used for throwing the pot. The potter should support the arms by pressing them tightly into the sides of the body whilst centring in this way. The centred form should have a narrow base to help define the bottom of the pot.

The bowl form being made has quite a narrow base, and lifting proceeds from this point.

The fingertips are used in all of the early stages with such a small pot, which requires a delicate touch if the form is to be made successfully. It is much easier to coax the bowl open with several swift movements rather than one strong pull; in this way a better feeling for the emerging form will be acquired.

A deep cut should be made with a rib at the base of the pot to define its bottom edge. A potential problem with making pots from the hump is lack of compression in the base, which can result in cracks, their distinctive 's' shape appearing when the pot dries. Particular care should therefore be taken to try and compress the base.

A twisted cord or thread with a toggle attached at one end only, is used for cutting off the pot. The cord should be wrapped around the deeply cut groove, and as the wheel revolves, pulled quickly through, resulting in a clean and level cut.

One of the easiest ways to lift a pot from the wheel is shown, using the divided first and second fingers of each hand.

Repetition Throwing

Making a number of pots of identical shape and size is known as 'repetition throwing'. As a means of production, repetition throwing is both versatile and efficient; moreover the skill required to make similar pots improves with practice, and speed quickly develops. The real advantage of throwing as a method of multiple production is that form can be readily changed or developed – a very costly thing to do when using moulds. The skilled thrower's limitation is how many pots one thrower can physically make in a day; studio pottery relies mostly on batch production rather than mass production, although historically it has been proven that wheel-made methodologies can be employed for producing in volume.

Learning to make shapes in an identical manner teaches the potter as much about refinement of form as it does about production. The familiarity of movements when making similar shapes develops into a rhythm that brings a confident character to a pot, and the established rhythm eventually becomes unforced so the potter can concentrate on the product and not just the process. It is perhaps not surprising to learn that most individual pots are actually made in series, and not just as 'one offs', the differences between a batch of four large bottles or jars being subtle, rather than extreme. There is also a certain satisfaction to be had from seeing a group of identical forms lined up on boards after a day's throwing.

Illustrated is a sequence of making a cup and saucer, items that are familiarly seen in groups, rather than individually. These shapes are good for a beginner to make, for several reasons. First, the basic bowl shape for a cup is quite within a beginner's capability. Also, making identical pieces will focus attention on the efficient distribution of clay during throwing. Saucers are simple flatware shapes, the challenge being manipulation of form, rather than process. Then the need for a cup handle will help develop the potter's repertoire of skills. Finally, to put all the differing elements of form together successfully requires a degree of understanding of the process of manufacture aligned with the demands of use and visual sympathy.

'. . . When the potter sits and freely throws the same items all day, and possibly day after day, it is only to be expected that the first will be stiff and self-conscious; but gradually throwing becomes free, and as the pots flow, forms take on a richness and vitality. When the potter is making 50 or 500 pieces of similar proportions he will naturally lose stiff intellectual thinking, leaving room for feeling and intuition to guide him.' Janet Leach.

Making a Cup and Saucer

Materials: Fine clay body:

BBV ball clay	75
Grolleg china clay	12.5
Nepheline syenite	12.5
Red iron oxide	1

Weight and thrown size: Cup: 350g (12oz); width 11.5cm (4.5in), height 9cm (3.5in) Saucer: 420g (14.8oz); width 18cm (7in)

In repetition throwing there needs to be a simple means of measurement that is easy to use. In this instance a wooden pointer has been set to measure the height and width of the pot simultaneously. The first pot is thrown, and measurements taken until it is the correct size; if the pot has been made many times before, familiarity with the form will make this an easy task.

In the first stage, the clay is generally distributed by throwing the wall up to meet the pointer.

Once the clay has been distributed, the form may be refined to the desired shape: achieving this depends on having an understanding of the form, rather than trying to copy a previously made pot. Understanding the rhythms of the form develops through repetition making, and often a few pots need to be thrown before this rhythm is established. Once it is, the process becomes a series of hand movements that automatically produce similar forms. Thus concentrating on the subtlety of the completed form is a better guarantee of making matching pots, than looking at previously made examples.

The problem with looking at previously made examples is they are in a different position to the one on the wheel and a false impression of the shape ensues.

The pot is cut from the wheel-head and lifted off, being careful not to stick the pointer into the clay; a pointer with a movable end is helpful. The cup must not be made too thin or it will distort in the firing from the pressure of the handle. A thick rim will be unpleasant to drink from, therefore it has been thinned slightly to provide a 'drinking edge'. If the clay wall is thinned subtly from inside to the rim it will appear to be a thinner, more delicate cup whilst retaining strength in the body of the form.

Clay is cut away to make a foot-ring: the fingers of the left hand pressing down hard on the pot enable considerable force to be exerted during turning without fear of the pot coming adrift. This will promote rapid turning, which is advantageous for both efficiency and aesthetic character. A cup's foot-ring must be relatively broad to aid stability, particularly on a wide breakfast cup such as the one illustrated.

It is sensible to wait until the cups are finished, complete with handles, before making the saucers; then a cup may be placed on a saucer whilst it is being thrown, and any modifications made. A rib is used to form the flat well of the saucer in which the cup will stand level.

It helps to turn on a pad of clay when making a group of pots of the same size: the pots drop into the indent made in the pad, and are held in place by exerting slight pressure. This method means that pots are quickly removed and replaced during turning. An additional advantage to turning on a pad is that the entire outside form of the pot is visible, which brings a greater degree of understanding of how turning is affecting the form.

The pad of clay should be beaten out with a dry hand so that it remains in a fairly dry condition. If the pad is too soft clay will adhere to the pot, causing unnecessary problems to remove.

The foot-well should be wider than the foot-ring in order to provide support for the cup without the drinker needing to be too accurate in locating it, tea drinking being a fairly casual social affair. To finish the edge of the saucer a chamois leather is used to promote a well compressed, slightly rounded edge that will take a good coating of glaze and be chip resistant.

The relationship between cup and saucer may be seen completely at this stage and adjusted if necessary. The space between the handle, with the fingers inserted, and the depth of the saucer is critical, and the design must allow for a finger to be placed under the handle as support without coming into contact with the saucer. This requirement needs to be balanced with the shape of the saucer, which should not become too flat, so that it can be picked up easily.

This complex but intriguing set of design issues presents a challenge that has many potential solutions, making the production of cups and saucers something that every potter should try. The finished cup and saucer made by the author is called a breakfast cup and intended to hold a large volume of tea or coffee. The design of the form places the handle quite high, so the hand can act as a lever when manipulating a full cup.

The crucial relationship between the handle and the saucer is controlled by the height of the foot and the angle of the saucer.

Making a Mixing Bowl

Bowl forms are the basis for many differing types of pot made for food. The mixing bowl, designed for preparing liquid foods such as beaten eggs, sauces or dressings, is particularly good for developing new skills since it incorporates a thickened rim, lip and handle. The challenge lies in the maker's ability to successfully unite the disparate parts and create something attractive to the eye, whilst producing a bowl that fulfils its practical requirements. These requirements are to accommodate the ingredients, and also contain them during the mixing process of whisking or beating; and the bowl's design must be such that it can be held and manipulated when full of ingredients with just one hand, leaving the other free to whisk, stir, mix and so on. The key elements of the design therefore require that:

- the proportions enable the pot to be held in one hand;
- the interior of the bowl is finished with an inturned rim to keep liquid contained during the process of whisking or beating;
- the handle is almost completely closed, designed to be gripped with the thumb over the top, giving control of movement whilst keeping the fingers and thumb out of the contents;
- the lip is broad, allowing a lot of liquid to be dispensed quickly and smoothly;
- the interior is curved, allowing smooth movement of a whisk.

Visually these elements are linked with a detail that exploits the characteristics of the materials and firing, to lighten what is potentially a quite bulky design.

Materials: Fine clay body, suitable for salt glaze:

Hyplas 71 ball clay   66 per cent
Grolleg china clay   33 per cent

Weight and thrown size: 900g (32oz) of clay; width 20cm (7.8in), height 8.5cm (3.3in)

Mixing bowls are best made in small batches, quickly thrown, the fluency of movement developing to give the forms their characteristic boldness. Centring, illustrated with one hand removed, reveals the distinctive mushroom shape that makes for quick development of the form. The fleshy part of the thumb presses downwards, and the fingers are arranged to pull inwards at the same time. Both hands carry out this action repeatedly during centring.

A very fast method of opening out continues, with the wall being lifted between the thumb and fingers. The thumb of the left hand hooks over the rim to stop it thinning too much. This method of opening is swift and potentially brutal, so care must be taken not to tear the clay completely from the wheel.

It is usually necessary to relubricate the hand during this movement as the clay can quickly become dry. A bowl shape is automatically established with this method of opening and subsequent lifting follows the curvature established at this stage, maintaining a good bowl form. Care must be taken not to thin the wall of the bowl at the rim as it is to be flattened.

Mixing bowl, by Alex McErlain. Width 17cm (6.7in). Salt-glaze stoneware, 1999. This pot, glazed blue and salt-fired, shows the effect of salt glazing, which bleaches the colour from the ridges formed on the rim, handle and lip.

The thick rim for the bowl is made in the early stages by pressing down with the index finger of the right hand whilst simultaneously gripping the wall of the pot between forefinger and thumb of the left hand.

The wall of the bowl is thinned by throwing up towards the rim, whilst retaining the thickened edge.

The thick rim may be detailed with a fingernail, the left hand supporting the wall of the pot to prevent it collapsing under the strain. A wooden modelling tool could be used instead of a fingernail.

When undercutting the base, always use a wooden tool as metal tools will wear the wheel-head unnecessarily. It is important to undercut at an early stage so that the form of the inside of the bowl is not disturbed.

In order to be able to pull a lip from such a thick rim, it must be thinned. The index finger is crooked to work the outside of the pot against the thumb inside, gently teasing the rim into a thinner wall. Lips may be pulled on almost any shaped rim if this method is adopted. The resultant lip will be raised higher than the rim and may help in balancing the design of the pot.

The lip is pulled by using the index finger and thumb of the left hand to define the width, whilst using the wet index finger of the right hand to stroke the lip from side to side until the desired shape is achieved. In order that the flow of liquid is cut off cleanly when the user stops pouring, the lip should flow smoothly from the inside of the pot and conclude without drooping.

Final adjustment may be made to the lip by pushing the rim back into the form. Clay will always move a little during later stages, as it has a memory for its original shape; the potter must therefore compensate for this movement at this stage.

The lip is raised higher than the rim of the bowl, so in order for the pot to be turned, it must be set on a ring of clay with a section removed. Centring the pot is tricky, as there is not much scope for moving it – a series of lines drawn into the pad may help in placing the pot close to centre.

A partially pulled handle is attached to the rim of the pot in preparation for pulling.

When pulling the handle, the pot must be held in the left hand so that the handle can be pulled downwards. Notice how the thumb is squeezing the clay whilst being supported on the back of the handle with crooked fingers.

The clay used for the handle of this pot was not in prime condition and has begun to split when bent to this extreme. I like to encourage this effect, however, because the detail marries well with the rim; but the risks inherent in achieving it means that a number of handles break completely when being bent into shape.

*R*ed lustre decorated bowl. Width 15cm (6in). Earthenware. Spain, eighteenth century. This simple bowl incorporating a clear glaze over white slip, has been decorated with copper lustre. The lugs are decorative as well as practical, and carry decoration from the inside of the bowl onto the rim. The three scars in the middle of the bowl are evidence of another pot being fired inside.

9 Making Lids

Lidded pots have a long history in wheel-made wares because of their capacity to protect stored goods, always a desirable factor. A lid will keep the contents of a pot from contamination, from being eaten by predators and from spillage during transportation.

There is much more to lidded forms than simple practical issues: the transformation in appearance brought about by fitting a lid onto a form has intrigued many potters, to the extent that the lid sometimes becomes the most important part of the object. Fitting a lid to a pot requires accuracy of throwing and a good understanding of the visual change the lid will make to the finished form. There are many differing types of lid, and quite a few solutions for making them. Most decisions about which type of lid to make are influenced by practical considerations: for example, a teapot lid must not fall off during use, and this affects its design; and a casserole lid is usually wide, which affects its behaviour during firing.

A lid will enclose the form of a pot both physically and visually, so it is important to consider the completed form when the pot is being made. The dexterity and accuracy required for throwing lids may be developed through making three simple types: a lid with a gallery, made upside down; a cap fitting lid, also made upside down; and a sunken lid, thrown the right way up. These three lid types may be adapted to make many variations in both form and fitting, and can lead to the exploration of a wide range of design ideas.

Lidded jar, by Richard Batterham. Height 31cm (12in). Salt-glaze stoneware, 1980. The lid has a broad flange that overhangs the form, whose simplicity is enlivened by a chatter-mark pattern. It is normal practice to make the lid after throwing the pot. The beginner may find it instructive to make more than one type of lid to fit into a gallery, thus understanding the change brought about by differing designs.

The Lid with a Gallery

A lid that incorporates a gallery is usually made upside down. The first stage is to make a shallow bowl with a flattened rim.

The rim provides the clay from which to make the gallery; this is split using the thumb of the right hand to press down whilst supporting with the fingers.

Once the gallery has been formed, the lid is thrown to size, and this necessitates being able to get the fingers well under the pot; with small lids this is made easier if they are thrown off the hump.

The inner measurement of the gallery should be taken, as it is easier to adjust the outer measurement during turning.

The forefingers of each hand are used to lift the pot off the hump; note the shell-like mark left by the cutting cord.

Lids made in this way are turned when leather hard, and have a knob or handle attached. There are other techniques for making this type of lid: a common method is to throw a thin bowl and fold the form back on itself to shape the gallery.

This produces a strong gallery made distinctive by the inner line created through the process. It takes a bit of practice to know how much to lift the wall of the bowl before folding it back on itself. Once mastered this method may prove to be easier when adjusting the size on a larger-scale lid.

*T*his lid slightly overhangs the body of the pot, always a more pleasing visual effect. If the point of contact with the pot is thin, the chances of the lid sticking during firing will be reduced.

*T*he pot has a gallery into which the lid fits. This is a very good design for teapots, as a catch to prevent the lid falling off during use is easily accommodated. Always take the measurement for the inner fitting, as it is easier to adjust the outer fitting through turning.

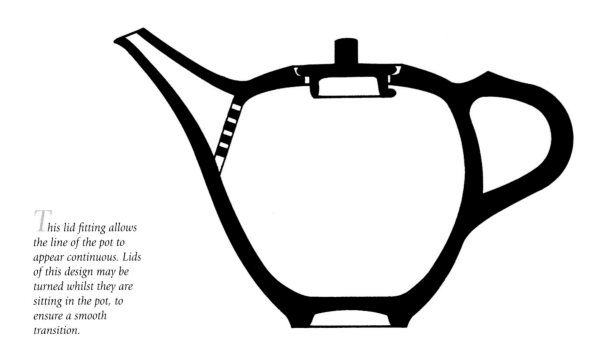

*T*his lid fitting allows the line of the pot to appear continuous. Lids of this design may be turned whilst they are sitting in the pot, to ensure a smooth transition.

'Leopard casserole', by Peter Dick. Width 34cm (13.4in). Wood-fired slipware, 1987. The lid of this English slipware pot has no gallery: it was made as a shallow bowl, and sits in a gallery on the pot. The modelled handle in the shape of a leopard provides a firm grip, well away from the hot lid.

The Cap Fitting Lid

A cap fitting lid is one of the simplest to make and has a dramatic visual effect on the completed form. The lid is made as a shallow bowl with steep sides, and the depth is critical as it should sit on the shoulder of the pot and not the rim.

The angle of the wall will considerably affect the finished form. Callipers should be inserted down into the bowl to ensure the correct measurement.

Some potters use a specially made wooden stick to take this measurement and ensure the lid will fit. When used on teapots, cap lids must take account of the steam that will condense on the inner surface of the lid. The condensation will run down the inside of the lid, then the outside of the pot unless a modification to the interior shape is made. Cap fitting lids may also be adapted to make a screw fitting.

OPPOSITE:

Bread crock, by Ray Finch. Height 37cm (14.5in). Reduced stoneware, 1973. Very large pots of this type require a lid that is strong in form so it is chip resistant; they must also be wide enough for the crock to fit a loaf. The strap handle echoes the form of the handles on the shoulder.

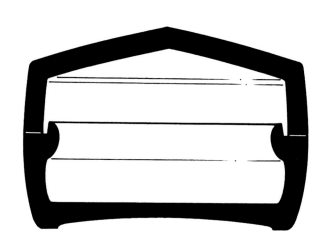

*T*he cap fitting lid should rest on the shoulder of the pot. It is important to taper the inner shank to prevent it from jamming if it is a close fit.

*S*mall boxes often incorporate this type of lid, as the shape of the box wall may be made with an uninterrupted form.

*T*his type of lid gives a false appearance of a cap fitting. The walls on the inside of the lid allow condensation to drip back into the pot. This type of lid is used on teapots to overcome the technical condensation problem whilst retaining the aesthetic appeal of a cap fitted lid.

Lidded pot, by Ray Finch. Height 10cm (4in). Reduced stoneware, 1974. This cap fitting lid is very appropriate for the chun glazed form, as the thick layer of glaze needs a simple surface on which to be seen to decorative effect.

The Sunken Lid

The particular advantage of a sunken-style lid is that the form is visible the right way up when throwing, thus allowing more control over the visual relationship with the pot. The shape has a low centre of gravity, which is useful if fitted to a teapot, as it will not fall off easily during use. Sunken lids are made from a hump of clay unless the lid is very wide – it is much easier to manipulate small amounts of clay off the hump.

A clay ball is opened, leaving some clay in the centre to form a knob. The knob is completed at this stage whilst it is easy to access; it may be thrown solid or hollow.

Patrick Sargent throwing sunken lids in his studio in Switzerland. The tapering column of clay will be used to produce a board full of lids. (Alex McErlain)

The remaining wall of clay is thrown out to form a shallow bowl; the edge may be turned downwards to make the surface for fitting. The angle at which this section is made must correspond to the angle of the fitting on the pot.

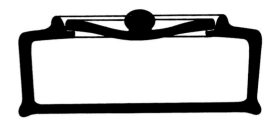

*F*itting a sunken lid into a gallery provides a very firm seating.

Sunken lids are measured across their full width to fit into a gallery or onto a rim.

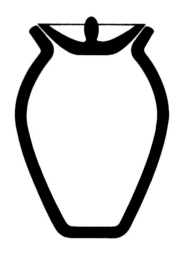

A sloping gallery fitting allows the lid to locate freely.

Turning a sunken lid must be carried out on a thick pad of clay with a hole cut in to accommodate the knob.

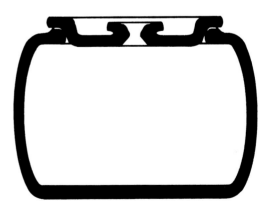

A slight overhang allows glazing to be taken right over the edge of the lid. If the knob is thrown lower than the rim, it will be possible to stack the pots, a useful design feature for casseroles. A broad lid of this type must be made on a batt.

*S*tore jar, by
Rosemary Cochrane.
Height 18cm (7in).
Salt-glaze stoneware,
1994. The lid sits in a
splayed gallery on the
pot with the knob rising
quite high. The
distinctive orange-peel
texture is an effect of
salt glazing.

Issues Related to Lid Making

Knobs and Handles

The knob or handle on a lid frequently plays a strong visual role in the design of the pot, and proportions may be exaggerated to enhance this effect without becoming too bulky. A knob can be shaped in many differing ways, and if it is to be added to the turned form, it is possible to try out a variety of shapes before attaching it. A thrown knob, formed by sticking a small ball of clay to the turned lid, allows the shape to be adjusted very easily. The completed lid should be put on the pot immediately to gain a clear understanding of the finished design. It is sometimes possible to throw on the knob whilst the lid is sitting on the pot, thus giving an immediate indication of the proportional relationships.

Drying Lids

Lids should be dried on the pot from the leather-hard stage until they have passed the point of warping, to ensure the fit remains accurate. If a lid is too tight to turn round completely in the gallery it can be slackened slightly by careful grinding of lid and pot together when they are dry. This process will, however, spoil the finish on the two surfaces.

Firing Lids

Stoneware and porcelain lidded pots are normally fired with the lid in place on the pot, as this helps to prevent the form distorting during firing, resulting in a lid that does not fit. Firing the two parts of a pot together also helps maintain an even colour match, as colour effects may vary in different parts of the kiln. Teapot lids need to be in place during a high temperature firing to prevent the pot from warping into an oval shape, caused by the weight of the spout and handle.

It is good practice to put a thin layer of alumina between fired surfaces to prevent them sticking: alumina does not melt at stoneware temperature, and so prevents the surfaces from sealing themselves together. The clay body will become slightly soft at very high temperatures as the clay becomes vitrified, and the presence of iron in the clay will cause lid and pot to readily fuse together if there is nothing to prevent this happening. When throwing the pot, keep in mind the surface the lid will touch, and try to keep the point of contact thin to help prevent adhesion.

Firing lids off the pot enables the gallery to be glazed. Earthenware is not as prone to warping, therefore many earthenware pots are fired without their lids on. This is beneficial to earthenware as the body would otherwise remain porous, and with use would not be very hygienic.

Wadding

In salt-glaze firings everything becomes glazed, and because of this pots must be set on wadding to prevent them sticking to the kiln shelf, or the lid sticking to the pot. Wadding may also be used if there is a danger that the glaze will run. It is composed of calcined alumina and china clay, sometimes mixed with a little flour to make it easier to use.

10 Plates and Dishes

Plates, dishes and shallow forms, known generally as flatware (as opposed to hollow ware), are quite simple to throw, nor is there much lifting involved in the process – but patience is necessary. The development of skills in making flatware is a good means of building confidence when learning to throw, and there should be no problems attached to gradually increasing the scale of the pieces tackled by the beginner, until they can manage a large dish, bringing with it the satisfaction of throwing a relatively large pot.

Design

A traditional plate will usually have a wide rim and a slightly curved centre, and the scope for design exploration lies largely within the proportional relationship of these two elements. The rim may carry some decorative treatment, the nature of which may influence its width. Plates used purely as vehicles for decoration – such as the slipware chargers of seventeenth-

Plate, by Ray Finch. Width 38cm (15in). Reduced stoneware, 1972. Ochre slip, poured and combed, covered with a white matt glaze.

century England – may be intended to be leant against a wall, or mounted on it, in which case the potter must consider how the plate will stand or hang. For instance, it will be much harder to make a plate with a steep-angled rim stand-up, than a relatively flat one. Wall-mounting plates by attaching wire hangers to the rim is bad practice as it often results in damage; a better solution is to make some provision with the foot-ring for holding a fixing device.

Dishes normally have a completely flat base combined with a shaped rim. The base proportion usually dominates and lends itself to decorative treatment. The rim of a dish will have to be raised in such a way that it may be grasped to pick it up, and therein lies the potential for the development of form and detail, which acts not just practically but visually as a frame for the central area.

Process

Batts

With flatware, the need for making on a removable batt must be considered at the outset: whilst it is possible to lift off a shallow form, distortion is almost inevitable. Very large batts sometimes exceed the width of the wheel tray, but it is possible to raise the batt on a thick pad of clay. A batt will also be used for inverting the plate without damaging the rim.

Centring

Most of the clay used in making flatware goes into the base of the pot, and a great deal of energy can be saved by beating the clay into centre before wetting it – it can be beaten into a shallow mound, or even a hollow ring, so that centring becomes not much more than smoothing out the form.

Compression

Opening up a large ball of clay to make a plate will leave the centre of that ball with little compression, and if the clay particles in the base lack compression, a crack with an 's' shape will

form as it dries. Any wide-based pot is susceptible, but plates are particularly prone to compression cracks. One solution for extra large plates is to throw a small lump of clay first into a flat sheet, then add more clay on top of this to continue throwing. Using a rib helps a lot with compression, though care must be taken to compress the clay, and not remove it.

Turning

The rim of a wide plate will dry much faster than the thick area of clay in the centre, consequently as the rim dries it will shrink faster, and in so doing will lift in order to accommodate the shrinkage. Care must therefore be taken not to allow the plate to dry too quickly, or the rim will develop cracks. Normally the rim is beginning to lighten in colour before a plate can be turned over to harden on the underside. Plates should be turned over by placing a batt on the top so that the pot is gripped between two batts: it may then be inverted, and in this way very little strain is put on the rim. The plate may be centred on the wheel whilst sitting on the batt, thus avoiding further damage.

The foot-ring must be cut deep enough in the centre to avoid the glaze touching the kiln shelf during firing. By holding a straight-edged ruler across the foot-ring, it is possible to gauge accurately the depth of the gap in the centre. Some plates with particularly wide feet are prone to droop in the firing; one solution with these is to leave a small 'button' of clay in the centre to provide support in the kiln.

Drying and Firing

It is vital to dry plates slowly in order to avoid cracks appearing in the rim. As a plate dries, it will undergo a lot of shrinkage, and if this is uneven it will probably warp, and splits will appear in the rim. If possible the plate should be kept upside down during the drying-out stage, as this will slow it down somewhat and help maintain flatness. Large plates should be bisque-fired standing on their edge and leaning against some kiln furniture (not the kiln elements). The reason for standing a plate up, is that a flat contact with a thick kiln shelf will cause heat to be retained in the centre of the plate for much longer than in the rim, and this promotes cracking.

Plates and shallow dishes offer much potential for decorative treatment. The process of decoration itself may also bring forward some practical design issues: for example if the pot is to be slipped, a groove made close to the rim may help to keep the slip within the inside during pouring. If the pot is to be hung on a wall, the foot may be turned outwards, or pierced to fit a hanger. Plain forms perhaps require a particular emphasis on the detailing of base, edge and rim.

The plate illustrated shows clearly the changes brought about by the application of different thicknesses of white slip, finger-combed to expose the darker clay body. The yellower colour near to the rim is a consequence of the iron glaze from the outside being picked up by the ash glaze within. The composition of fluid movement in pattern and glaze is made effective by keeping the form very simple. The colours work particularly well when the dish is filled with fruit, because as the fruit is removed, the pattern plays an increasing visual role – so effectively the dish never looks empty!

Making a Plate

Materials: Clay body:

Hyplas 71 ball clay	40
Hymod AT ball clay	40
Fine silica sand	8
Molochite	5
Grog 30/85	7

These proportions make a body with a good texture and colour, suitable for throwing large forms. The clay responds to bold treatment, the filler ensures low shrinkage, and the colour is effectively complemented by white slip.

Weight and thrown size: 3.5kg (7.7lb) clay; width 34cm (13in), height 8cm (3in)

The process of plate making begins with attaching a batt to the wheel-head so the pot may be easily removed when complete. There are a number of different ways of fixing batts; the method illustrated, showing six pieces of clay

Fruit plate, by Alex McErlain. Width 29cm (11.4in). Reduced stoneware, 1995.

stuck to the wheel-head, is a simple one, although it does have the disadvantage that the pads have to be replaced if they are removed when lifting the batt off. A more stable method is to lay a pad of clay down and make the surface of it sticky but not wet.

The batt should be clean and dry to adhere well, and hit firmly in the centre to fix it down.

Check that the batt is revolving true, and is not tilted. If working on a pad of clay, it is a good idea to fix the first batt down before wedging, then it has a chance to stick well. Damp the surface of the batt before fixing the clay; the lump must be compressed into a wide, flat shape when centring, and this is achieved by pushing down with the palm of the right hand whilst simultaneously compressing with the palm of the left hand.

A lot of energy may be saved if the clay is gently beaten into shape by patting with the palms of both hands whilst the wheel revolves slowly, in this way the large lump of clay can almost be centred before finishing off in the conventional manner. It is also possible to beat out the clay into a wide open ring or doughnut shape before wetting and centring the ring which is relatively easy to do. Very large plates are best approached in this manner. Beating out the clay helps to compress it better than conventional centring methods, thus minimizing the risk of compression cracks.

To open a hollow shape, push down with the wrist, compressing downwards as well as pushing out.

Before opening out the base completely, it is worth checking the thickness by pushing in a fine spike and measuring the depth with your finger.

The base of a wide plate should be made slightly thicker than normal to allow for the cutting wire, which will make the clay thinner towards the middle. At this stage it is easy to adjust the thickness. The clay is then drawn outwards with both hands, using a pulling motion,

until a thick ring of clay is left for making the wall at a later stage.

With wide-bottomed pots it is important to compress the base to prevent cracking. The cracks that result from a poorly compressed base have a distinct 's' shape, and may not appear until the pot has been fired. Compressing and smoothing the base begins by using the fingers to press down and push outwards from the centre.

When the base is complete, the wall may be thrown from the ring of clay left earlier. On this pot the rim is compressed between thumb and fingers, leaving a slight in-turn that will help at a later stage with slipping and glazing. The pot should normally be cut off at this stage and lifted with the batt. The batt should be levered gently from the wheel-head, taking care to avoid sudden movement, as this could make the rim collapse. Sometimes, with very large plates that are going to be coated in slip, it is helpful to delay cutting the pot off until it has been slipped, so the plate is held by the batt.

Patrick Sargent made numerous plates; he would set them in his kiln in stacked-up fashion, keeping them separated by the use of clay-filled seashells. In his own words:

> Sometimes shells are used just for decorative effect. In this plate [overleaf] the four marks in the middle have come from sea shells filled with wadding, placed the right way up. The white mark is caused by alumina. This plate was made using the throwing technique of adding a coil on for the rim which has been rolled out unevenly so that when I throw it out again it doesn't actually come out perfectly round, giving a free and wavy quality, softening the perfect circle of the plate and

The base should also be compressed with a rib, held in both hands and moved outwards from the centre.

marrying sympathetically with the shape. The indentations are filled with chun glaze that tends to pool out. I like fluid glazes, ash glazes and chun glazes, all of which can dribble all over the place. The secret is to learn how to use them so that you have a good success rate at the end of the day.

The plate is decorated when leather hard, before turning, with a thick layer of white slip. Note that when pouring in slip the jug is held completely over the plate so that it catches any drips.

The slip is swirled around gently whilst holding the plate by the batt and rim. The slip will make the base very soft, so turning must be delayed until the following day, by which time it will have rehardened. (Note that if the base had been turned hollow before slipping, the foot would have collapsed as the clay softened.) When the slip is poured out, the slightly in-turned rim helps to define how far up it has been poured.

Slip must be cleaned from the rim quickly before the clay softens; once the wet slip has begun to stiffen slightly, a pattern is finger wiped through it. The action of finger wiping will push some slip into a thicker layer, and this will affect the character of the ash glaze used on this plate.

P late with four shell marks and chun-glazed spots, by Patrick Sargent. Width 35cm (13.7in). Wood-fired stoneware, 1991.

Oval Dishes

There is a strong historical tradition for making oval or squared dishes, which continues today; perhaps it is the generally accepted, powerful circular appearance of a plate that invites distortion to produce a completely different effect. It is possible to make a dish oval by removing a lozenge-shaped section of clay from the middle of your circular shape, and then rejoining the two sides. This is the traditional method of making oval dishes, which dates back several centuries, and there are other related techniques that achieve a similar result.

Squared forms can be achieved simply by pushing the sides of a steeply walled dish. A plate rim can be cut into flat sections to bring about a contrast between the circular middle and the faceted edge. Attaching handles to the rim of a dish will also visually reconfigure the form.

When a dish is made oval through distortion the angle of the wall changes. It is common to see oval dishes thrown with quite steep-sided walls as the walls lean outwards when reshaped, producing a much shallower form. Oval dishes should always be dried out slowly to avoid cracks appearing as a result of the serious tensions set up during the process.

A plastic comb marks the final details. It is interesting to observe the difference in character between the finger-wiped lines and the combed ones.

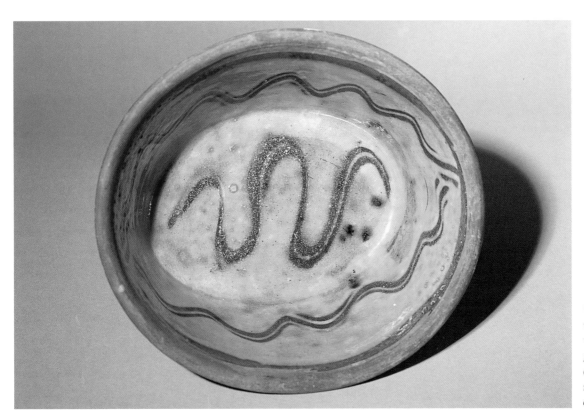

Oval dish, made at Winchcombe pottery. Width 25cm (10in). Earthenware, 1930. Combed white slip over red clay with a yellow-coloured lead glaze.

Slipware plate, by Peter Dick. Width 31cm (12in). Wood-fired slipware, 1983.

Featured Artist: Peter Dick

Traditionally English slipware used a repertoire of techniques, a way of working first developed in the seventeenth century; it is continued today in an entirely contemporary manner by the studio potter, Peter Dick.

Working in the village of Coxwold, Yorkshire, Peter makes good use of flatware to develop decorative slip techniques. Slipware application methods mostly result in soft, thickened lines, so the decorative patterns and motifs must work with this characteristic. The decoration on this plate combines the slipware techniques of trailing, brushing and finger wiping. Peter fires his kiln with wood, consequently the fire modifies the glaze and body, softening the colours and speckling the clay.

Peter works with a red clay body which is very plastic. The clay has a considerable effect both on the forms he makes and the decorative surfaces. The pots must take into account the fact that they are to be coated with a layer of slip; the substantial rounded edges help in this matter, producing part of the recognizable language of form which Peter has developed.

11 Jugs and Pitchers

A good pitcher is the most lively and athletic of all pots, realizing the conjunction of grace with strength, ready and apt for action yet majestic in repose.

Michael Cardew, *Pioneer Pottery*

Jugs or pitchers are particularly challenging to make: they must be thinly potted so they are not heavy to pick up; they must pour well; the proportions are frequently tall and narrow, making it difficult to lift the clay in the early stages of throwing; and they need to incorporate a pulled lip, and a handle that is effective to use: all these factors contribute to the challenge of designing and making a good jug. The design factors should not be seen as constraints, but as a challenge for the artist to be inventive whilst fulfilling the practical demands of the pot.

Numerous forms have been adapted to make both useful and expressive jugs, and there are so many differing possibilities, so many historical solutions to reference, so many practical uses each with its own demands, that it is no wonder that potters are eager to master the art of making a jug.

Purpose

Jugs are a common household item, and come in many sizes and shapes: tiny ones for cream or milk, pint jugs used for measuring, coffee jugs, pitchers for holding flower displays, and very large ones, the largest often being purely decorative. A jug's purpose may be quite specific, as for example the oil pot made by Sidney Tustin at Winchcombe Pottery illustrated overleaf. This jug is fitted with a stopper, it has a tiny pouring lip that dictates a fine flow of oil,

and the scale relates to its use on the dining table.

Quite different practical factors need to be considered in the design of the lidded coffee jug made by Ray Finch. The open spout of this jug allows for a generous flow of liquid, the pot will be hot in use so the handle must accommodate a firm grip without burning the fingers,

Ash-glazed jug, by Alex McErlain. Height 29cm (11.4in). Reduced stoneware, 2000.

*O*il pot,
Winchcombe Pottery.
Height 15cm (6in).
Reduced stoneware,
1973.

and the lid, which helps retain the heat in the coffee, must not interrupt pouring. Frequently jugs are non-specific in their purpose, but still demand a good relationship of balance, pouring, grip and stability.

Scale

When considering design ideas, the scale of a jug may influence some decisions. The one pint jug made by Richard Batterham illustrated overleaf is grasped with the index and middle fingers inside the handle, the thumb on top and the other fingers below to act as a lever. The form with its narrowing neck allows the fingers

to be positioned away from the pot in case the contents are hot. The placement of the handle is quite high, consequently the pot is stabilized in use, with a low centre of gravity. The wide base provides stability, and the thickened rim protects the edge from chipping during casual use on the table. As may be seen, there were several factors that needed to be taken into consideration when the pot was being designed.

There are other elements that have influenced the decisions about form. The pot is covered with an ash-based glaze, whose characteristics are enhanced by the way the form is manipulated: for example, the tendency of the glaze to run a little is controlled by the thickened rim, the incised lines around the middle, and the deeply scored handle. The fluid glaze

ABOVE LEFT:

*O*ne pint jug, by
*Richard Batterham.
Height 13.5cm
(5.3in). Reduced
stoneware, 1974.*

ABOVE RIGHT:

*J*ug, made in Cologne.
*Height 20cm (8in).
Salt-glaze stoneware.
Eighteenth century.*

OPPOSITE:

*L*arge pitcher, by
*Michael Casson.
Height 46cm (18in).
Salt-glaze stoneware,
1984.*

gathers at these points, and glassy pools of glaze contrast with the brown edges of the raised lines. Batterham, like many British potters, admires the jugs made in mediaeval England, and the essential characteristics of this simple, useful pot have their roots in mediaeval English pottery.

Expression

The decision to make a monumental jug or pitcher is frequently influenced by the opportunity to develop decorative characteristics within a large expanse of form. A pitcher is defined by Hamer as a 'large jug intended for carrying and storing liquid' (*The Potter's Dictionary of Materials and Techniques*). The pitcher made by Michael Casson was thrown in two parts. The rounded base was made first and left to stiffen, and then a partially thrown neck was attached and re-thrown. The extremely thick rim of the pot has been pinched out to form the lip. A rounded handle complements the rounded nature of the pot, and accommodates all the fingers, giving a sturdy grip. The decoration is made by the potter drawing his fingers through wet slip, producing marks that complement the curvaceous form and add a sense of movement. The pitcher has been salt-glazed, resulting in a variety of surface textures, depending on the thickness of the slip. Casson has made hundreds of jugs and pitchers, and enjoys the challenge of exploring form and decoration within the complexities of the design requirements.

Salt glazing originated in Germany, it is carried out by introducing salt to the hot kiln when the temperature is in excess of 1200°C. The salt, which is sodium chloride, breaks down into a gaseous state and moves around the kiln where the sodium combines with the alumina and silica in the clay to form a thin skin of glaze. Some of the characteristics of Casson's pitcher may be seen in the salt-glaze jug made in Cologne; the rounded form of the handle and the blue decoration are typical of German pottery.

Making a Jug

Materials: Clay body:

Hyplas 71 ball clay	40
Hymod AT ball clay	40
Fine silica sand	9
Molochite	4
Grog 30/85	7

This makes a body with a good texture and colour, suitable for making larger forms. The clay will stand up well during throwing because it has a high content of coarse material.

Weight and thrown size: 2.7kg (6lb); height 30cm (12in), width 14cm (5.5in)

The clay ball for this jug has been kneaded into a cone shape that is thrown onto the centre of the wheel-head. This shape helps with the first stages of centring. The pot is being made on a batt to facilitate removal.

The first stages of centring involve pushing inwards with the palms of both hands simultaneously. With a larger piece of clay it is important to centre parts of the lump, rather than all of it at the same time. Notice how the arms are resting on the wheel tray to give a strong support to the pushing movement.

The clay is being centred by pushing downwards, the right arm crooked, the elbow raised, to exert pressure downwards, starting at the top and moving down the lump of clay to the wheel-head. The left hand pushes inwards to maintain control of the centred form.

The jug is to have quite a broad base, so the centred ball of clay is left wide at the bottom.

When opening out a larger ball of clay with the thumb, it helps to press down with the thumb of the left hand on top of that of the right hand; note the fingers of the right hand pointing towards the body. This is a fast and effective method of opening; however, there is a limit to the size of the ball that may be opened out in this manner.

When pulling open the form, the fingers of the left hand are positioned inside, working with the right hand compressing the clay from the outside. The left hand thumb is wrapped over that of the right hand, giving a very strong grip and helping to maintain control of the emerging ring of clay.

As the base of the jug is completed, it appears wider than is necessary at this stage. With the pot opened wide, it is easy to compress and finish the base completely. Good base compression is essential to avoid cracks appearing in the latter stages of drying.

The first lift is made using the side of the right hand to push upwards and inwards. This is a very powerful grip, and care must be taken not to rip the clay off the wheel-head; take it slowly.

Lifting the wall with the side of the knuckle of the right hand, the thumb of the right hand is used to support the clay as the lift progresses. This technique is sometimes known as the 'pistol grip' because of the arrangement of thumb and crooked fingers.

The knuckle exerts a powerful grip enabling a good amount of clay to be brought up from the base fairly quickly, the wider contact with the clay which the thumb brings giving additional support during this aggressive movement. It is helpful to raise the clay into a cylinder quickly so the pot does not become too soft with continuous lubrication.

When completing the first stages of lifting, the form is concave, because this is the easiest shape to maintain control of. The rim must be kept under control at this stage.

Lifting continues and shaping begins by using the flat area between the first and second joints of the index finger to support the wall on the outside whilst pushing from the inside.

The rim of the jug is detailed with the fingertips, affording it a strong but visually light characteristic. The deep-cut rim will support a thicker pool of glaze, bringing about a change in colour.

At this stage the final touches are made to complete the pot: the surface is now free of excess slurry; final adjustments are made to the form; clay has been removed from the base; and a deep undercut has been made. The jug will not be turned, so it is important to see the finished form at this stage. The undercut at the base of the jug casts a shadow that helps to visually lift the form. It also provides a convenient point to which to clean back glaze at a later stage.

On this pot, shaping is finalized by using a rib that removes most of the throwing lines left by the fingers, and which compresses the thin wall of clay.

It is possible to pull a lip straight onto this type of rim; alternatively the rim is thinned as shown by gripping with the thumb and crooked forefinger to coax the clay into a gentle curve.

The rim is now ready for forming the lip.

When pulling a lip, fix its width with the thumb and forefinger of the left hand whilst shaping it with the right forefinger. The finger should be wet, and a movement made from side to side whilst pulling from inside the pot to the outside. The action of cutting off a flow of liquid without it dripping is helped if the lip is relatively thin and the angle at the tip points slightly upwards. Drooping lips are prone to dripping.

The finished jug, ready for removal from the wheel-head, has been cut off the batt with a wire; the batt will be gently prised up, avoiding any sudden movements that may distort the form.

Pulling a Handle

If a handle is required, the thick slug of clay for making it is held in the palm of the left hand whilst the right hand manipulates it. It helps to keep the left hand dry to give grip, and to constantly wet the right hand to facilitate smoothing and thinning. The handle shape is formed at this stage by squeezing between thumb and fingers.

A length of clay, slightly longer and thicker than that intended for the final handle, is prepared.

In preparing the pot for pulling a handle, a section of the rim is scored deeply where the handle will join: water is used to work up a slurry that will help the clay adhere.

Gripping the slug of prepared clay with a clean, dry right hand, the handle is rammed firmly onto the pot. This will form a really strong joint if done correctly. If you examine shards of broken jugs, look at how invariably a section of the pot rim is still attached to the handle, proving the strength of the joint.

The clay is nipped off carefully on a clean, dry board, the thumb being used to cut downwards.

Pulling the Handle on the Pot

The best way to control the visual relationship of the handle to the pot is to further pull the handle when it is attached to the pot, thus enabling a high degree of control and adjustment to the design.

The handle is pulled with both hands. On a large form the pot will be heavy enough to hold its position; smaller pots may be held up to allow the handle to be pulled downwards, working with the forces of gravity. Note how the fingertips support the gripping action of the thumb, which has been crooked to give a pincer-like grip. This process must be carried out swiftly.

The handle is bent and brought to the bottom of the jug to be attached. At this stage adjustments to the size of the gap for the fingers can be made easily.

Final adjustments may be carried out to moderate the curve, and test out the potential for gripping.

When pressing home the clay to attach the base of the handle, it is important to spread some of the clay outwards rather than cut it all away, otherwise the resultant handle may appear visually weak. There are many ways to detail the base of the handle, from smoothing it into the form, to developing elaborate decorative treatment.

At this stage the handle is quite soft and will move easily, sometimes not holding its adjusted shape because of the softness. If this is the case the pot should be left for an hour when the clay will have stiffened a little and adjustments may be still made. This is the moment to add thumb stops or fill in the base detail with a fillet of clay.

This jug is being dipped in white slip to provide a different surface for the glaze to react with. The pot is in a good, leather-hard condition and may be safely gripped, in one hand, at the base. By monitoring the position of the base in relation to the surface of the slip, a level dip is achieved.

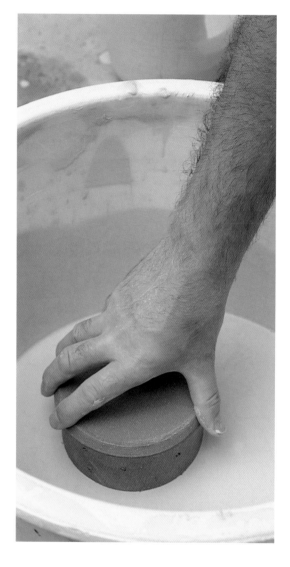

When lifting a pot out of the slip, pause to allow any excess to drip off; try to keep the pot moving gently from side to side to facilitate this. The jug may be turned upright with a swift motion of the arm. It is a good idea to practise this action before you dip the pot in slip. The pot must only be slipped on one surface at a time – in this case the outside. If both surfaces require slipping, the inside should be left to reharden before slipping the outside, otherwise the pot will become too soft and may collapse.

Featured Artist: Jim Malone

Jim Malone is renowned for his jug-making capabilities, and his range of designs includes all the classic forms. He particularly admires medieval English jugs, and frequently references them when discussing ideas. His admiration for the pots is centred on their inventiveness and their origin; he sees them as part of an indigenous culture, to which he is proud to belong.

The ideas for detailing the jug opposite were inspired by medieval pottery. The decorative application of pellets of clay, the base of the handle filled with a small fillet to add visual strength, the cutting of the neck to open a pouring hole for the applied 'beak'-shaped lip, are all found in those inspirational pots produced in medieval England.

Malone's cut-sided pitcher illustrated overleaf was designed to make the most of the particular characteristics of an ash glaze; its expressive nature of casual but accurate throwing and cutting is heightened by the glaze characteristics. In the words of Malone himself:

Ash glazes began, as I'm sure every potter is aware, quite accidentally in the East when it was observed that wood ash falling on the exposed ware during firing formed a crude glaze. It was a fairly obvious next step to apply wood ash deliberately to the pots before placing them in the kiln, and an equally obvious second step to try mixing the wood ash with some other material. This was initially no more than the clay body itself, and a little later, whatever clay or stone was locally at hand. In this way, the glaze was no more than a reorganizing of the materials and processes already in use, and is therefore not foreign to the pot in any way, just a natural extension of it.

Beak-lipped jug, by Jim Malone. Height 21cm (8.2in). Reduced stoneware, temmoku glaze. 1990.

Cut-sided pitcher, by Jim Malone. Height 37cm (14.5in). Reduced stoneware, 1994.

12 Teapots

Bernard Leach's comment on the troublesome nature of teapots is in stark contrast to the statement made by Geoffrey Whiting, who was renowned for making teapots. The teapot has been widely used as a vehicle of expression,

> 'A teapot is a difficult thing to make well; yet partly because of this, and partly, I think, because the teapot is such a deep-rooted integral part of our daily lives, few things can give a potter more satisfaction.' Geoffrey Whiting, *Pottery Quarterly*, 1955.

attracting the attention of both maker and user to unusual forms that serve the purpose of pouring tea whilst simultaneously making a visual statement.

When tea drinking was first popularized it was an expensive luxury, and the utensils associated with it were required to have an appropriate character. In the twentieth century, tea became a very cheap drink, and mass-produced teapots such as the ubiquitous 'Brown Betty' served a utilitarian demand; but there continued to be a market for unusual design. Studio potters found people prepared to pay sometimes very large sums of money for a teapot, so

Teapot, by Alex McErlain. Height 22cm (8.7in). Salt-glaze stoneware, 1997. This teapot has been fitted with a cane handle fixed into modelled lugs. The faceted spout and sgraffito lines animate the glaze, which helps to pull the composition together.

'A teapot is about the most difficult article a potter is called upon to make. ...it will be readily understood that tea sets involve the studio potter in troublesome and unremunerative work.' Bernard Leach, *A Potter's Book*, 1940.

there continues to be an interest in developing new designs.

Many teapots of distinction are purchased in order to build a collection, rather than to be used, and this seems a pity when the maker puts so much effort into ensuring the pot functions. The intrigue of teapot function is perhaps the reason that most potters want to try making one at some time in their lives. Geoffrey Whiting gave helpful advice for those considering making teapots, in an article published in 1955. It was seen as a defining point in communication about the process, and inspired many others to make teapots. The teapot fulfils a commonplace role in society, it is the epitome of an everyday object, yet to make one that works successfully in a practical, as well as an aesthetic sense is a difficult thing to achieve.

Design

The complex arrangement of disparate elements presents a challenge to the designer of a teapot. The design must integrate practical as well as visual issues, deal with scale and context, whilst taking into account the behaviour of the clay through the making and firing process. Drawing is a good way to approach teapot design, as it helps to visualize the finished object, and highlights some of the decisions to be made that will affect it. Teapots are slow to make and assemble, therefore drawing affords a much quicker means of initial design development; however, drawing cannot resolve all the problems, and it is important to make and remake a design in order to see clearly the subtle changes that are necessary if you are to produce a successful pot.

A successful teapot design is usually developed slowly, through evolution rather than revolution. Teapots that are used as an everyday item may have particular characteristics defined by their context. For example, a small teapot used in a cafe may be of an appropriate size for a single customer, holding enough tea for two cups, and it may have a certain robust character so as to withstand frequent use.

A lex McErlain, teapot design ideas.

Whatever the criteria, the designer must resolve all the issues to produce a practical and attractive pot.

Purpose

There are many practical factors to be taken into account when designing a teapot.

The Shape of the Body

Many shapes are viable for teapots, some easier to deal with than others. Concave shapes are the most difficult to fit a spout onto, although they will accept a handle easily. The base of a teapot should suggest stability in use, but this does not necessarily mean that the pot should be wide-bottomed. Final decisions about form should not be made without first considering how the fittings will change it.

Lids and Galleries

A lid serves the purpose of keeping tea hot in the pot; it also plays a significant role in the composition of the form. Some lids are made to sit in a gallery, perhaps the most common method of completing a teapot body. One advantage of a gallery is that it is easy to make a catch fitting to prevent the lid falling off. A gallery on the pot body also helps keep a high-fired teapot in shape during the firing when the spout and handle are exerting pressure to distort it. Sunken lids have the distinct advantage of a low centre of gravity that makes them difficult to dislodge during pouring. Cap fitting lids look good on many forms, however, they must have a device in the inside of the lid to prevent the condensed steam from running down the outside of the pot during use.

Handles and Spouts

The fitting of a handle and spout does more to change the character of the design than any other aspect of a teapot. Spouts have limitations in scale that do not necessarily relate well to the scale of the pot body. Thus a very large teapot will not work well with an oversized spout because the control of flowing tea must relate to the teacup into which it is being poured. Side handles must be proportioned in relation to the user's hand, so the pot is easy to manoeuvre but without burning the fingers.

Teapot with a pulled side handle for a right-handed person, made by Patrick Sargent. Height 13cm (5in). Wood-fired stoneware, 1993. Pulled or thrown side handles are common on Eastern teapots; however, they always restrict use depending on which side of the pot they are pulled. The spout should be placed at slightly less than 90 degrees to the handle to make pouring easier.

Pulled overhead handles are easy to use during pouring because the weight is distributed in a balanced fashion below the hand; however, draining and cleaning is made more difficult, because the handle restricts access to the inside of the pot. Cane or wire handles are a good compromise because they may move to allow access. Thrown or pulled side handles placed at 90 degrees to the spout are distinctly left- or right-handed, depending on which side they have been fitted.

With so many practical considerations to take into account, it is not surprising that developing a design for a teapot is seen as one of the greatest challenges in the art of throwing.

Throwing a Teapot

Materials: This is a fine-grained clay body composed of:

BBV ball clay	75
China clay	12.5
Nepheline syenite	12.5
Red iron oxide	1

Weight and thrown size: 800g; height 13cm (5in), width 13cm (5in)

Teapots may be thrown quite quickly, since they are composed of only a few small thrown parts that are fairly easy to make. However, the time taken to assemble a teapot is far greater than the throwing time, and for this reason it is important to make only as many pots as may be completed the following day. The beginner will probably be able to complete a batch of six teapots within a day, a number that will still enable him to develop fluency from the familiarity of the repeating process. In production making, when all the decisions about design have been extensively developed over time, and the potter is totally familiar with both form and process, the quantity may be increased in relation to the individual's speed of making.

The Body and Gallery

When throwing teapot bodies, the need to shape the lid fitting must be taken into consideration during the early stages of making. The body of the pot must be able to support the pressure exerted when the gallery is being

made without distorting; it is a good idea to form the gallery at an early stage. Here, the flattened rim of a thick-walled cylinder is split to form a gallery.

A balance must be struck between the need to form the gallery early and the difficulty of shaping the body of the pot once the gallery has been formed. It is possible to continue lifting and shaping the body without distorting the gallery on a fairly large teapot, but on the smaller sizes the potential for distortion is high.

The thumb of the left hand divides the rim by pressing down, whilst the fingers and thumb of the right hand give support. Once the gallery has been formed, the body of the pot may be shaped, taking care not to deform it; fingers may be tucked under the gallery to develop the round shape of the body.

The Lid

A lid is made by throwing from a hump of clay. A small portion of the hump is centred in a distinctive, mushroom-like shape.

A pair of callipers are used to measure the lid fitting.

The lid to fit this pot will have a gallery, so the innermost measurement is taken. If the lid were to be of the sunken type, then the wider gallery measurement would be taken. The teapot has been thrown directly onto the wheel-head, and may be easily lifted off.

Teapot bodies are very enjoyable to throw, the bulk of the finished shape of the teapot is largely complete at this stage and it is possible to visualize what the completed pot will be like. Uppermost in the imagination is the positioning of the teapot spout that will have to be fitted. Many teapots incorporate a straight area on the form in anticipation of where the fittings will be placed; this also helps in forcing a space to occur on the shoulder where the shape changes towards the gallery as the shoulder will need to be wide enough to take some types of handle fitment.

It is quite important to keep the base narrow to aid removal from the hump. The first stage in making a lid is to form a shallow bowl with a flat rim that is split with the thumb of the right hand to form a gallery.

The lid may then be thinned out to the correct size by throwing the clay from the centre to just under the gallery.

The Spout

Spouts are also made from a hump, as it is much easier to work with the clay raised above the wheel-head. To make a spout, a small cone shape is opened up: notice how the fingertips are used for lifting when working on this scale.

The importance of having a narrow base becomes obvious in this illustration. The lid should be measured across the narrowest part to fit the pot.

A small lip is pulled on the lid to form a catch that prevents it falling off when in use.

The shape should taper smoothly from base to tip, and is finished by working up and down the surface to smooth the curve that will aid the flow of tea.

The catch will fit under the gallery of the pot. A hole must be cut in the lid to let air in when pouring tea. The hole may be cut adjacent to the catch, in order for the pourer to recognize its position when the pot is in use.

It is important to carry out this process gently to avoid putting too much stress on the form: this will manifest itself later, through twisting. At this stage the spout is made longer than will be required. Also it may be left straight, or it can be bent into a different shape prior to removal.

The spout is cut off with a single-ended cord, and lifted with the fingertips of both hands. Quite large pots may be lifted off a hump of clay in this way.

Assembly

Turning the Body and Making a Foot-ring

Teapots are usually turned whilst sitting in a chuck, as the top of the pot is relatively narrow in relation to the form, and would be difficult to fix to the wheel-head. The chuck is fixed to the wheel-head with a pad of clay.

This teapot is to have a foot-ring thrown on to it, a technique that facilitates making a deep foot without having to turn away a lot of clay. The pot is prepared by scoring and wetting the area to take the coil.

A coil is added to the base of the pot and pressed firmly down.

By using a wet natural sponge to press down and centre the coil, very little water is used and the main body of the pot remains dry.

The foot-ring is then cut away to form the feet.

The foot-ring is left to dry a little before cutting commences, to avoid cut pieces of clay adhering to the freshly thrown foot. The foot-ring is marked out to ensure the cutting is divided evenly; later it is necessary to see that the feet coincide with the placement of the spout.

At first it is cut quite roughly, then gradually refined, and finished with a wet finger to smooth the cut surfaces.

Completing the Lid

The lid is turned on a soft pad of clay, the centre being scored with the turning tool to affix the knob.

Teapot on feet, by Michael Casson. Height 12cm (4.7in). Salt-glaze stoneware, 1986. The high feet on this small teapot are used to develop the wavy line decoration and add a sense of balance to the form, which could otherwise appear top heavy because of the handles and knob detail. This teapot also makes use of a bent spout.

A small piece of clay is pressed onto the centre of the lid to form the knob.

This technique helps with deciding how big to make the knob, as differing sizes may be tested prior to fixing. The knob is easily centred. Its form must be shaped so the lid can be removed easily when the pot is hot, without burning the fingertips.

The form of the knob makes a contribution in detail to the overall image of the vessel; many variants in design are possible. This teapot has a lid that sits on top of the pot, rather than in a gallery.

Fitting the Spout

One of the most difficult tasks in teapot making is fitting the spout. It is helpful to hold the spout behind the body of the pot in such a way that it is possible to envisage it attached, and so make a decision about the angle at which to cut it.

The spout is cut cleanly with a thin-bladed knife, whilst resting it on the wheel-head.

It should be held against the pot to see how it relates to the form, whilst decisions are made about placement, which must also take into account the flow of liquid.

The tip of the spout must be at least as high as the top of the body to prevent the tea coming out whilst the pot is being filled. The visual arrangement of the parts is perhaps the most complex thing to get right at this stage.

The spout has been wetted and held briefly against the pot: this leaves behind a mark that shows where the grid is to be cut. When cutting the grid with a hole borer, use a finger inside the pot to support the thin wall. There must be a greater total area of hole at this end of the spout than at the other end, otherwise the tea will not enter fast enough to make it pour well. The pot is scored and wetted; usually by this stage it is getting quite hard.

The spout is pressed firmly onto the body, and the join modelled in.

Some potters try to model the spout so that it appears to blend smoothly into the form, whilst others emphasize the join. The end of the spout may be cut, enabling it to pour well, cutting off the flow of tea cleanly without dripping. As the spout has been thrown into a very narrow form there is tension in the clay that will make it twist in the firing. All narrow-necked pots twist, but of course we do not usually notice the result. If a teapot spout is cut level and twists it will end up crooked, so it must be cut at an angle to allow it to twist into a straight position. The easy way to remember which way to angle the knife is to hold it in your right hand with the spout pointing away from you, and cut towards the thumb as if peeling a potato.

In this position the angle should lean down to the side that is holding the knife – in other words, to the right. This rule relates to pots thrown with the wheel revolving anti-clockwise.

Now most of the teapot is complete; most potters will put the lid on the pot at this stage to get acquainted with the nuances of the form and anticipate the type and placement of the handle. Beginners should spend time thinking about the change the handle will make at this stage. It is possible to roll out a coil of clay and mock up various options to get an idea of how the form changes, and anticipate the challenge of manipulating a pulled handle. For cane handles the actual cane can be placed on the pot before the lugs are attached and for pulled overhead handles some stiffened, previously pulled shapes will help to try out possibilities. Once the decision has been made the pot must be brought to the right condition to accept the handle. By this time most bodies will have dried considerably and may benefit from a light spray of water to bring the clay back into workable condition.

Pulling a Handle

It is quite a challenge to pull a handle on a teapot successfully; the pot itself is difficult to hold in one hand, and the handle must be pulled quite long to make it big enough to accommodate the fingers.

The pot must be raised and angled to allow the handle to be formed. A teapot handle must be able to accommodate several fingers, whilst keeping them away from the hot pot.

At this stage it is possible to test out the shape of the handle and make some adjustments. A full teapot may be quite heavy, and the thumb usually plays an important role in gripping the top of the handle.

Teapot with two handles, by Ray Finch. Height 19cm (7.5in). Reduced stoneware, 1990. The second handle on this large teapot enables the weight to be carried by two hands, giving an added degree of confidence to the user. The pot has been dipped in an iron-bearing slip that was combed whilst wet. Dipping teapots in slip is a risky business, since the thin spout and large handle are both vulnerable to cracking if they are not in the correct leather-hard condition.

Featured Artist: Will Levi Marshall

Will Marshall has always made unusual teapots. The challenge of developing an interesting new form within the parameters of a functional object characterizes his approach to making. The distinctive features of the teapot illustrated overleaf, with its slabbed spout and curved base, are emphasized by the use of several differing glazes. The spout has a sharp angularity that is echoed visually in the treatment of the base. These angular shapes are in contrast to the soft forms of the body, handle and knob, the entire form held together visually by the use of layers of glaze. The handle protrudes over the gallery to form an effective lid catch. Some of the influence for the design of this object may be seen in Japanese Oribe ware.

Teapot, by Will Levi Marshall. Height 12cm (4.7in). Oxidized stoneware, 1994.

Teapot, by Will Levi Marshall. Height 24cm (9.4in). Oxidized stoneware, 1998.

With this teapot, the spout has been made from a sheet of clay that is rolled and joined before modelling onto the pot. Moulded spouts avoid the problems of twisting that occur in thrown ones, and allow the potter to make a wider range of shapes. The overhead handle gives effective control when pouring, as the weight is distributed below the level of the hand. One drawback with pulled overhead handles is the difficulty in draining the pot upside down after rinsing it out.

13 Bottles and Jars

The production of bottle and jar forms for the transportation and storage of goods occurs in many civilizations throughout the history of wheel-made pottery. The practical nature of the shapes – with a narrow neck through which to pour and contain liquids, or an open cylindrical form to store materials – produces forms that lend themselves to expressive development. Forms may be seen as bold, plain shapes, possibly with anthropomorphic references –

foot, shoulder, belly, for example – or as a vehicle on which to develop ceramic decoration in all its guises. This expressive potential of the form has produced many pots whose sole purpose was expression of idea rather than practical use. Not surprisingly, many studio potters continue to explore the expressive potential of the bottle and jar.

Making a bottle is a fairly straightforward, though skilful matter. Essentially a bottle is a closed-in cylinder that may be made in one piece by progressively narrowing the form to make a neck. The technical challenge of preventing the form collapsing during the final stages requires economy of movement during the early stages of lifting so the clay does not get too wet and overworked. Quite large bottles may be made in one piece, and undoubtedly the control of form is easiest if changes may be made to the entire pot during throwing. This chapter will feature makers who have made bottles and jars in differing ways, rather than trying to show, stage by stage, the many variations in approach to making and modifying bottles.

Jim Malone is known for making bottle forms that are often used as a vehicle for developing ideas suggested by the characteristics of slip and glaze. For example this tall, slender bottle has been coated with coarsely brushed white slip. The technique of coarse brush work is known as 'hakeme', and the brush marks emphasize form in a stark, austere manner, drawing attention to the graceful profile. The proportional relationship of the narrow neck to the widest parts of the form is significant in the way we read this form. In making the bottle the clay was initially lifted in a concave cylindrical shape to attain the necessary height, then the cylinder was gradually coaxed out to form the gently swelling shape.

Tall bottle, by Jim Malone. Height 42cm (16.5in). Reduced stoneware, 1998. Hakeme brushed slip under a clear glaze.

Process

Throwing Necks On

Bottles are easier to form if the neck is made as a separately thrown addition; in this manner the pot may also be made much larger, without the struggle of coaxing the clay during the last stages of throwing. A neck can be made by adding a coil of clay when the pot is leather hard, and throwing it on the pot. It is common practice to partially throw a thick ring of clay instead of making a coil; re-centring is made somewhat easier in this manner.

The practice of making the body and neck in two completely separate parts requires a really good perception of the completed form, and is usually undertaken when other methods are deemed impossible. The potter Lucie Rie frequently made pots with a separately thrown body and neck; in the illustrated example the two parts are joined at the shoulder. The bottle is made from agate, an incomplete blend of differing clays, and reveals a spiral pattern developed as a result of throwing. Pots such as this, with a very long neck, are difficult to control if made in one piece, the weight of the neck putting a lot of strain on the shoulder below. Making in two parts is not just a problem-solving solution, but brings further creative potential through developing forms, that may be impossible to make in any other manner.

Flattened Bottles

Bottles lend themselves to distortion by flattening with a paddle into squared or oval shapes. When a narrow-necked bottle is pressed into a shape with flattened sides, the visual emphasis of the form is shifted. The shoulder becomes very prominent, emphasized by the change in direction caused by flattening; the pot has distinct 'sides' that may be decorated as panels, and the surface is altered during the flattening process.

The proportions of the flattened panels bring another strong visual element to the form, sometimes dominating and at other times complementing. The flattened bottle made by the author, illustrated overleaf, has two panels that emphasize the roundness of the form with its curvaceous neck and foot.

To make a flattened bottle the form may be coaxed into shape when it is leather hard. If the bottle has been made with a separately thrown neck it will be helpful to wait until this, too, has become leather hard before beating the pot. Sometimes the flattened shape may be initiated during throwing by pushing with a finger vertically down the inside of the pot, thus turning the major part of the form into a non-round shape. With dexterity the potter can continue to throw the neck, and later, a foot-ring may be turned to complete the pot. The paddle with which to beat a bottle can contribute texture to the faceted surface. Some potters use a heavy piece of wood to flatten the form, whilst others hold the pot and tap it on a bench to achieve the required shape.

gate bottle, by Lucie Rie. Height 36cm (14in). Oxidized stoneware, 1967.

*S*quared bottle, by Jim
Malone. Height 30cm
(11.8in). Reduced
stoneware, 1996.

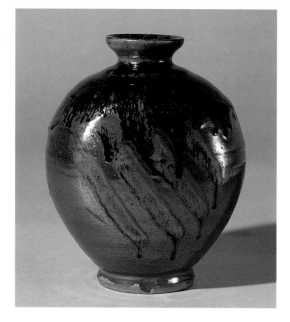

Flattened bottle, by Alex McErlain. Height 21cm (8in). Reduced stoneware, 1997. Glazed with ash and iron glazes.

Techniques for Making Large Bottles and Jars

Large pots are not only a challenge to make, but are inevitably striking to look at because of the way they dominate space. There are many techniques for making big pots, and it is worth noting that you do not have to be a large, muscular person to be successful in this! Most very large pots are made in stages, a section at a time, which is also allowed to dry; work can then progress without risk of the pot collapsing. The techniques of coil and throw, or joining partially thrown sections, are common ways in which potters make big pots.

Pots made in sections or stages have a different character as a consequence of the process of making. The asymmetric shape of the enormous bottle made in France brings life to the form, making it appear very human with its variety of lumps and bumps. The potter was undoubtedly skilful enough to overcome these apparent imperfections – but perhaps we must assume they were not seen as imperfections at all.

The process of coil and throw is common in Asia and has been copied by many studio potters who want to make big pots. Large jars, such as the one illustrated from South-East Asia, are begun by throwing a bowl from about 14kg (30lb) of clay. When the bowl is leather hard, about five coils, weighing 9kg (20lb) in total, are attached to the rim, then thrown to increase the height. This process continues until the pot is of the required size. The form is then consolidated by beating – that is, holding a block of wood inside the pot and hitting the outside with a wooden paddle. This is known as a 'paddle and anvil' technique. The pot must stiffen

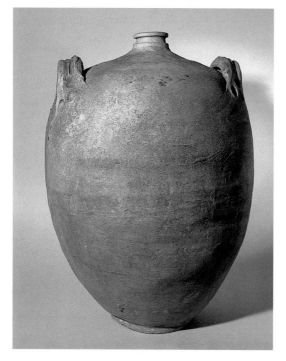

French bottle. Height 62cm (24in). Nineteenth century.

Large jar from South-East Asia. Height 45cm (17.7in). Stoneware, buff clay with two slips, dark under light, roulette decoration. Nineteenth century.

*P*ainted jar, by Robin
Welch. Height 69cm
(27in). Oxidized
stoneware, 1987.

between each stage of making. Pots made by coiling and throwing are best made in series so that whilst one pot is being worked, another may be drying.

There are many variations of the coil and throw technique, from throwing one coil at a time, to building partially by hand, thus making a pot that is a cross between a thrown form and a hand-built one. The jar made by Robin Welch is an example of a pot with both thrown and hand-built characteristics. Welch has built up the pot with hand-built sections on top of a large, thrown base, and allowed the shape to undulate, providing a three-dimensional canvas onto which he has painted slips and glaze.

Joining partially thrown sections together enables large jars to be thrown with a degree of continuity of form. The best way to achieve this is to throw a base section first and allow it to stiffen slightly before joining a second section and rethrowing the two sections as one.

Developing the Form with Additions

Large pots frequently have additions in the shape of handles or lugs, which help to punctuate the form. The additions may be purposeful, as in the cider jar that would be carried to the farm where cider was made, for replenishing. The handles on the large French pot could not be used to pick it up when it was full, as it would be extremely heavy – but they may have been used to help tip it over. Whatever their practical purpose, they make a considerable visual impact on the form, being placed directly on the shoulder of the pot.

The visual impact made by adding handles or lugs is commonly used by artist potters to develop distinctive form. In the jar made by Rosemary Cochrane, the handles have been added to make direct reference to the anthropomorphic characteristics of the pot – indeed, the base may be described as a 'skirt', with the entire object conjuring up an image of a woman with arms akimbo. This referencing of the human body is commonly seen in pottery, though not always in such an overt manner.

The handles placed on the jar made by Josie Walter illustrated overleaf are definitely not intended to be practical: they are small in scale, and have the purpose of helping to divide the form into two movements, drawing attention to the lower part to counteract a visually top-heavy shape.

On the lidded jar made by the author, illustrated on page 157, the handles are described as ears: they are purely visual, and serve no practical purpose. Historically in pots of this type, the handles were used to tie on a lid or to hang the pot up.

Sometimes the addition of elements with which to develop the form is taken to an extreme, the additions dominating to such an extent that the pot becomes a completely different object. In the bucket pot made by Patrick Sargent, illustrated on page 158, a complex set of references are used. The handle dominates the pot: it is made of clay and wood, and is pegged as if it were held together by the wood – although of course this is impossible, and the pegs are a false addition. The form is so tightly waisted that efficient pouring would be impractical, which contradicts the bucket reference; but these elements make us question how we see an object, and in the end the object is quite compelling; perhaps it is an object about the language of use.

Handled jar, by Rosemary Cochrane. Height 23cm (9in). Salt-glaze stoneware, 1997.

OPPOSITE:

Cider jar, by Michael Cardew; made at Winchcombe pottery. Height 37cm (14.6in). c. 1933

OPPOSITE:

Jar, by Josie Walter. Height 29cm (11in). Earthenware, 1997.

Lidded jar with ears, by Alex McErlain. Height 31cm (12in). Salt-glaze stoneware, 2000.

*B*ucket form by
Patrick Sargent. Height
30 cm. Wood fired
stoneware. 1990.

14 Composite Pots

The degree of control over form is seriously compromised when pots are made from sections, so composite forms are usually objects that cannot be made in any other way. The most common reason for making a composite pot is to achieve a larger scale than is possible from making a pot in one piece. There is also the potential for developing ideas that celebrate the very nature of joining separately made elements in an unusual form. This final chapter features the work of two contemporary potters who are renowned for making composite pots: Will Marshall and Kate Bartle. Will uses the technique to produce large stools, a pottery form with a long and neglected history; Kate, a potter with a passion for colour and texture, uses it to make double-skinned vessels that also have many historical precedents. These two young potters are exploring new ideas that recognize the importance of the historical context in which their work belongs.

Will Levi Marshall: Making a Stool

Will Levi Marshall is well known for his production of elaborately glazed tableware of distinctive form. The idea of making a stool first came to him after seeing one that had been made by Michael Cardew, and he began making stools himself when studying at Alfred University, in North America. Initially he made them in one piece, gradually evolving the idea into the form shown here, which in essence is composed of two upside-down pots joined together.

The time involved in making a stool is spread over several days. Initially the thrown parts for a batch of two or three stools will be made. During the following days the parts will undergo a sequence of cutting, distorting, turning and strengthening, before finally the two halves are joined together. It is vital to allow the parts to dry slowly between the stages of production; normally it takes four days from beginning to end, depending on the warmth of the workshop.

Black composite form, by Hans Coper. Height 31cm (12in). Oxidized stoneware, 1967. This form has a historical precedent in pilgrim flasks. Coper has successfully assembled a group of wheel-made forms into a new configuration with a distinctly modernist character. The stark black finish on this pot serves to emphasize the contours and the proportional relationship of the parts.

S tool, by Will Levi Marshall. Height 50cm (20in). Oxidized stoneware, 2001. (Will Levi Marshall)

Dimensions: Weight 15.5kg (33lb) for each section.

Body recipe:

Hyplas 71 ball clay	40
Grolleg china clay	40
Potash feldspar	15
Flint	5
White bentonite	1
80s molochite	5
120s molochite	15

The first stage of making involves centring a large amount of clay by beating three separate 5kg (11lb) sticks of clay together onto the wheel-head. The clay comes direct from a de-airing pug mill, and is not wedged. With a batt fixed to the wheel-head to facilitate removal, the process begins by beating down the clay stick with the side of one hand.

The clay is compressed in layers, and the rhythmic movement of hand and wheel ensures that the lump of clay arranges itself close to centre.

Will works on a Soldner electric wheel – 'the best electric wheel I've ever used' – that has no drip tray. Lifting such a large ball of clay requires the side of the right hand to push hard against the outside of the wall; close positioning of the body helps to provide the necessary leverage.

When roughing out the shape Will uses a crooked knuckle to lift the clay. It is vital to check the diameter of the base at this stage: 'If you don't get it fairly close now, you are doomed!'

When finalizing the shape he uses a sponge to wet the outside during lifting. The form is smoothed with a rib to get rid of throwing lines; his pots have complex glaze decoration that is more controllable on a smooth surface. The base of the stool will be formed from this section. At this stage the top curve seems to look ridiculously large, but its scale diminishes once the pot is assembled. The difference between scale and proportion is one of the prime issues when making composite pots. The scale of the rim may appear too large when it is being made, but its proportion in relation to the complete stool will be appropriate.

Strips of clay must be added to the inside of the pot as strengthening supports to prevent distortion during firing.

The base section of the stool is allowed to stiffen for a day until it will bend without collapsing. The pot is bent in three places to form what will become the feet of a three-legged stool.

The top of the stool is also thrown upside down: this complex form is illustrated clearly in the cutaway section. The seat of the stool is formed from the base of the thrown pot, the handles are cut below the rim, and the top of the pot is thickened to form the section that will join to the base.

Small additions of clay are made to allow adjustment, and to form stable feet. The pot will sit better on these clay additions which can be readily manipulated to ensure that the stool is level. Note how the edge of the pot has been left with a thick rounded section to make it less vulnerable in use.

The top section of the stool is thrown on a batt and must be allowed to stiffen until a fine knife can be used to cut through the pot at an angle of 45 degrees; this produces four slits, from which the handles will be shaped.

The cut has to go in at an angle because of the shape of the inside of the pot. The next stage is to push the pot gently in: it must be in a good, leather-hard condition otherwise it will slump inwards.

The finger holds are smoothed to prevent sharpness when in use. The finished section must be allowed to stiffen considerably before being turned upside down (or is this the right way up?) for the finishing process.

The rounded rim of the stool is turned and smoothed, a hole is cut in the centre, and the base pushed in gently so that water will drain if the stool is used outside.

Composite Pots

It normally takes three days' gentle drying before the sections are in the right condition for assembly. The stool is assembled upside down to enable access to the inside for joining the parts. With the two surfaces that are to be joined scored and slipped, the parts are assembled.

The central joint must be made strong so the stool does not break: good compression is therefore vital from both sides.

Will uses a spirit level to ensure the pot has not bent during assembly; minor adjustments are still possible at this stage.

The finished stool will be dried very slowly, as so many complex tensions have been set up in the clay, it may easily warp.

*P*ilgrim flask, by Jim Malone. Height 33cm (13in). Wood-fired stoneware, 1997. This pot was made by joining two concave bowls to construct a convex form with neck and foot attached, and it makes direct reference to pilgrim flasks that were made to be strung from the waist, or hung from a horse. The formal 'language of construction' of pilgrim flasks has attracted many twentieth-century studio potters, who have created their own versions of the form.

Kate Bartle: Making a Double-Walled Bowl

Kate Bartle has built a reputation for making composite forms from bowls that explore geometry, texture and colour. Inspired by the possibilities of contrast created between surface and form through the motion of the wheel, her pots are cool, poised and precise. The precision of the form and decoration is contrasted with a coarse, imprecise glaze. When lit properly the pots show her fascination with the interplay of colour and texture, their glistening surfaces revealing gem-like qualities. The bowls appear to be very heavy, but reveal a surprising lightness that is important to the artist.

Dimensions: Large bowl: 3kg (6.6lb); width 33cm (13in), height 16cm (6in)

Small bowl: 600g (21oz); width 16cm (6in)

Body: 'Craft Crank', a commercial clay body with a high grog content, firing a warm, toasted colour in an oxidizing atmosphere, selected for its colour, strength and capability to cope with the stresses from the composite making process.

The component parts for making a double-walled bowl consist of a small and a large thrown bowl, together with a rolled clay slab that is laid into a concave, bisque-fired mould.

The bisque-fired mould has a very shallow curvature. It will be used to support the pot during making, the porous bisque stopping clay adhering and allowing precision cutting to be carried out without damage to the mould's surface. Bisque moulds are much more durable than plaster and are usually made from red earthenware clay as it has a high degree of porosity when fired, combined with strength, which white clays sometimes lack. There is an additional benefit from Kate's use of this mould in that she can control the degree of curvature with precision, an important factor if the surface is to end up virtually flat after firing.

The bowls are thrown on a tile batt that is set in a holder (note the tile is fixed to the holder with small pieces of clay).

The large bowl is not cut from the batt, as this will be used to grip it when inverting. The first task in assembly is to set the small bowl upside down onto the slab, fixing it firmly. The slab sits in a clay mould attached to the wheel-head.

The larger bowl is inverted and joined after carefully scoring and slipping the edge.

The bowl is cut from the tile, and left to stiffen before turning.

The pot must be dried gently before cutting away the surplus clay from the rim using a sharp knife.

The pot remains supported by the bisque mould throughout the process.

Next, a hole is cut in the base with a sharpened stick;

this hole allows air to escape when the pot shrinks. When it is firm enough, the pot is turned the right way up on the wheel, and a pilot hole is made in the centre. Kate places her hand inside the pilot hole to guide the final cut.

The pot is then cleaned up and left to harden; at this stage the top is slightly domed, but it will drop in the firing. Decorating begins by setting the pot on the wheel-head in an off-centre position to enable a circular line to be drawn in the clay.

More circular lines are drawn using a protractor and a flexicurve;

the lines will be used to mark the position of a silicon carbide slip painted to the outside with a brush.

The slip is made from the clay body, with 5 per cent of fine silicon carbide added. During the firing the silicon carbide will cause the glaze to bubble with escaping gases, thus producing a crater glaze finish. The glaze brings out a reddish glow in the clay, and softens just enough to be gentle to touch.

The bowl is fired to 1,270 °C in an oxidizing atmosphere; during firing the top drops slightly until it becomes flattened. After the firing, a layer of gold leaf is applied. Special glue is painted on to take the leaf: this is pressed down with a sponge and left for one hour; any loose particles are then removed with a brush. Kate chose the glaze for its 'gorgeous colour and its ability to bubble with silicon carbide'. The glaze inside the pot has metallic characteristics that work well with the gold leaf, and contrast with the crater glaze.

Glaze used over the slip:

Soda feldspar	33
Barium carbonate	25
Dolomite	12
Ball clay	7
Quartz	7
Zirconium oxide	15
Copper carbonate	2

Glaze for the inside:

Nepheline syenite	73
Dolomite	5
Whiting	4
China clay	4
Bentonite	3
Flint	8
Zinc oxide	3
Rutile	10
Ilmenite	10
Copper carbonate	4

In Conclusion

Composite forms bring new possibilities to the art of throwing, developing interesting and unusual shapes that are as challenging to conceive as they are to execute. By making new ideas in series it will be possible to explore subtle changes of form, proportion and surface within the composition. Hans Coper was noted for making pots in groups or series, many of them composite forms. The pots were notable for the subtleties developed through making the same form with variations over and over again in a seemingly inexhaustible creative manner.

OVERLEAF:

Spherical form with flattened cylinder, by Hans Coper. Height 28cm (11in). Oxidized stoneware, 1967. The body of the pot is a large, thrown sphere to which a separate cylinder has been attached when flattened. The textured surface has been worked with layers of slip and engobe.

Glossary

anagama A single chamber kiln.

alumina One of the constituent parts of clay; it does not melt at stoneware temperatures.

ash glaze A glaze made using wood ash, usually combined with some clay.

bisque The first firing that renders pottery stable yet porous, to enable glaze to be applied.

blunger A machine for blending clay into slip form.

bentonite An extremely plastic clay of volcanic origin.

Cantigalli An Italian factory that specialized in the reproduction of classic Renaissance majolica wares during the nineteenth century.

chuck A support vessel for use during turning.

chun glaze A blue glaze that develops its colour through very thick application.

colloidal slip A slip of exceedingly fine particle size.

cross-draught kiln A kiln design in which the fire travels horizontally across the pots to the opposite end of the kiln.

de-airing pug mill A machine for mixing clay that also removes air.

earthenware Low fired pottery normally in the range between 1,050–1,150°C.

fly ash A kiln fired with wood produces ash that enters the kiln, flying around and landing on the pots.

frit A glaze material that has been melted and reground to render it insoluble.

filter press A machine for extracting water from slip under pressure to produce plastic clay.

flywheel A heavy wheel that, when set in motion, will continue to spin under its own momentum.

grog Fired and crushed clay used as an additive to pottery bodies.

leather hard The condition of clay when some, but not all of the moisture has disappeared.

lathe A machine for turning clay pots in a horizontal position, mostly used in mass production.

lustre A metallic surface on a glaze developed from metal oxide.

lead glaze A low-temperature glaze incorporating lead as a flux.

metal oxide A chemical combination of an element (metal) with oxygen. The metal oxides are used as colorants in ceramics.

oxidation firing Firing pots in an atmosphere rich in oxygen, as in an electric kiln.

porcelain A white clay body that contains a lot of flux to enable it to become vitreous and translucent.

pigment A mixture of metal oxides used in decorating pots, for example a mixture of iron oxide with cobalt oxide will produce a muted blue pigment.

pilgrim flask A bottle with handles used for carrying drinking water or holy water during a pilgrimage. The flasks normally have two handles, and are usually flattened in shape.

plasticity The condition of clay that enables it to be changed in shape easily and without fracturing.

raku A type of very low-fired pottery.

reduction During firing, a kiln may be starved of air so the flame still burns, but with a reduced supply of oxygen. This has an effect on the colours of clay and glaze.

refractory Material that is resistant to high temperatures.

stoneware High-fired pottery, usually vitrified, normally in the range between 1,250–1,350°C.

shard A piece of broken pottery.

slurry The thick, liquid clay produced as a consequence of throwing.

slip A liquid condition of clay.

torque A force that causes a rotation movement.

vitrification The point at which a clay body begins to melt before distortion begins.

vitreous slip A slip mixed with materials which help it to begin melting.

wadding A mix of materials that will not melt at high temperatures; it is used to support pots in the kiln, and prevent them from sticking to each other.

Bibliography/ Further Reading

There are numerous books available to help develop knowledge of the subject of throwing. Those listed provide an introduction to differing aspects of the subject and will help develop a broad knowledge.

Charleston, R., *World Ceramics* (Hamlyn, 1968)

Cooper, E., *Ten Thousand Years of Pottery* (British Museum Press, 2000)

Cardew, M., *Pioneer Pottery* (Longman, 1969)

Clark, G., *The Potter's Art* (Phaidon, 1995)

Eden, V. & M. *Slipware* (A&C Black)

Freestone & Gaimster, *Pottery in the Making* (British Museum Press, 1997)

Hamer, F. & J., *The Potter's Dictionary of Materials & Techniques* (A&C Black, 1975)

Leach, B., *A Potter's Book* (Faber & Faber, 1940)

Leach, B., *Hamada Potter* (Kodanshka, 1975)

McGarva, A., *Country Pottery* (A&C Black, 2000)

Manners & Morley-Fletcher, *Ceramics Source Book* (Grange books)

Mellor, M., *Pots and People* (Ashmolean Museum, Oxford, 1997)

Rackham, B., *Medieval English Pottery* (Faber, 1948)

Scott, D., *Clays and Glazes in Studio Ceramics* (Crowood Press, 1998)

Recommended Periodicals

These periodicals contain a wealth of information and are a prime resource for keeping up with developments in contemporary pottery.

Periodical	Country
Ceramic Review	UK
Ceramics Monthly	USA
Ceramics Art and Perception	Australia
Ceramics Technical	Australia
Ceramics in Society	UK
Studio Potter	USA

Yellow-glazed bowl, by Lucie Rie. Width 17cm (6.7in), height 9.5cm (3.7in). Porcelain, 1968.
The high foot on this bowl may have been made by throwing it onto the leather-hard pot. The severe form is emphasized by the distinctive yellow glaze that has a pitted surface texture.

Index